RESOURCE MOBILISATION FOR NGOS IN THE DEVELOPING WORLD

CURRENT AND EMERGING PRACTICES

Published by
Adonis & Abbey Publishers Ltd
P.O. Box 43418
London
SE11 4XZ
http://www.adonis-abbey.com

First Edition, March 2013

Copyright © Mavuto Kapyepye

British Library Cataloguing-in-Publication Data
A catalogue record for this book is available from the British Library

ISBN 978-1-909112-25-4

The moral right of the author has been asserted

RESOURCE MOBILISATION FOR NGOS IN THE DEVELOPING WORLD

CURRENT AND EMERGING PRACTICES

Mavuto Kapyepye

Adonis & Abbey
Publishers Ltd

Acknowledgements

The project of writing this book came about following encouragement from various people I have interacted with in my career and I would like to acknowledge their contribution abundantly. The journey that started as a post graduate dissertation research was made easier by Mr Marcel Chisi, Executive Director for the Active Youth Initiative for Social Enhancement (AYISE) of Malawi, who supported me in utilizing his organization as my case study. My former classmate at university, later a close workmate and still a close professional buddy Dr Chiku Malunga gave me inspiration many times through our conversations and his own books. I would also like to thank Maria Mhandire working for DHL for her insights into the private sector perspective which became a vital part of the authorship of this book.

I am also grateful to the following NGO leaders for sharing with me their experiences and insights: Ms Mary Malunga, Ms Maggie Kathewera Banda, Mr Jimmy Katuma, Mr Sam Kamoto, Mr McLean Sosono, and Mr MacBain Mkandawire. To my longtime friend Charles Gawani, who was always on call with insights based on his experiences in the NGO sector. I am also indebted to my very good friend Francis Mathero Malunga, who took the time to proofread and edit the manuscript. Your effort was not in vain. My gratitude also goes to Ms Linly Litta-Clayton for the logistical support in the UK.

The following people also provided wonderful contributions during the writing of this book: Dr Steve Waddell, and from BRAC, Sumaiya Haque, Tasfiyah Jalil, Pushpita Alam and the management of BRAC including Chairman Sir Fazle Hasan Abed.

Due credits have been made to all sources of case studies that have been adapted for use in this book.

Dedication

I dedicate this book to a bright future for my children Murendelhe and Oriihana.

Foreword

Mavuto Kapyepye has captured the essence of both how to fundraise and also, critically, the danger of being too reliant on a small donor pool, even if budgets are being met. This complacency has been the downfall of too many non-profit organisations.

Mavuto's passion for the non-profit sector shines throughout this excellent book. Fundraising/resource mobilisation is not just another job - it needs passion - the passion in compassion - Mavuto clearly has it.

As a fundraiser for over 25 years, I was most heartened to see the vital importance of social enterprises covered. Fundraising is merely one way to resource an organisation - social enterprises are the most important and dynamic development in the sector - ever. The more income non-profit entities can earn, make or generate, the less they have to raise, thus securing their own financial self-sustainability.

This invaluable book is brought to life and made more real by the fascinating case studies from developing countries around the world. It is a pleasure to endorse this outstanding work- the non-profit sector in over 100 developing countries need more people like Mavuto Kapyepye.

Jill Ritchie
CEO Papillon Press and Consultancy, South Africa
Former Vice President of the Southern Africa Institute of Fundraising (SAIF),Author of 26 books including many guides to fundraising

Preface

This book though primarily written for indigenous NGOs in the developing world, is a practical resource for all nonprofit organizations (NPOs) including University Trusts, faith institutions among others.

Financial sustainability and its associated autonomy do not appear on the priority list of most NPOs that are established especially in the developing world. However, the NPOs the bulk of which are NGOs, soon realize that having steady sources of funding is such a significant issue they cannot do without. Currently most of them are pressing panic buttons.

Suffice to say that when we are in the panic mode, our thinking is negatively affected and it is not easy to focus on our endeavors. Consequently, this limits our choices or there are none at all in terms of where and how we source funding for our NGOs and as a result we become vulnerable to manipulation. This is not the kind of situation we would like to find ourselves in yet most of us are already there and struggling.

Some of us are about to close shop because all the funding taps have dried; yet this is what we never imagined when the funds were flowing and the spending euphoria took the better of us. Others are winding down and worrying over the imminent loss of employment because the project is coming to an end and the NGO cannot retain us without the required project funding. Therefore, we must be asking ourselves as to what went wrong. For those who are still enjoying funding, this is the time to ask the question "what can go wrong?

Worthwhile to mention that most NGOs depend 100% on sources of funding they do not and cannot control and this brings an element of vulnerability because the decisions are made somewhere in an office overseas by decision makers who are detached from our context. Usually the decisions are abrupt. Is this the scenario we would like to continue in our NGO? Certainly this is not the kind of situation we would like to experience?

Is there a way NGOs can cushion themselves against such donor financial shocks? This book takes you through the process of answering this question in the affirmative. It takes you on the journey of trials and tribulations most indigenous NGOs in the developing world face, shares insights on the way forward and illuminates the areas that your NGO has control of and must work on and those that your NGO does not have control of but can and should influence. Based on practical experiences with resource mobilization practices from various parts of the world, the thesis of this book is that indigenous NGOs in the developing world should have a good level of leverage in their interaction with donors if the challenges raised in chapter one as experienced by such NGOs are to be managed strategically.

The purpose of this book is not to encourage NGOs to turn away from donors, but rather to advocate for a relationship that is based on mutual respect through a good understanding of the functionality of the NGOs in developing countries and why the donors tend to adopt the posture discussed earlier. This book is promoting a healthy balance between donor dependency and financial autonomy through the culture of entrepreneurship and professionalism among NGOs in the developing world.

May your resource mobilization drive enjoy a new lease of life!
Mavuto Kapyepye

TABLE OF CONTENT

Chapter One

The Dilemmas and Challenges in Resource Mobilization For Local NGOs in Developing Countries

It is Tuesday evening, 19th September 2006 and I am seated in my living room watching the evening news bulletin on TV. Marcel is an executive director of one of his country's outstanding youth NGOs and appears on a news item where he makes the following statement:

> It is important that Donors should listen…when we ask for money to promote poverty eradication to enable us fight HIV & AIDS better, instead of insisting on giving money for AIDS awareness…beyond awareness people need to see a practical link between HIV & AIDS and their livelihoods'.

The scenario above is a reflection of the flagship of this chapter. It takes you through the journey of dilemmas and challenges that an overwhelming number of NGOs in the developing world go through in the business of soliciting aid. It gives an insight into their daily struggles by way of highlighting "a day in the life of a manager of an NPO".

Most NGOs ideally work with disadvantaged communities to facilitate the process of improving their livelihoods as their primary objective. On the one hand the NGOs are closer to the people and better positioned to understand the challenges that their constituent groups face. On the other hand donors who usually do not have this knowledge keep the keys for the purse and hence they hold the power to influence their grantees. Managing the delicate balance of the sometimes bipolar demands is a daily struggle and this scenario places NGOs in a dilemma.

However, even in situations where donors have funded a project that truly responds to the needs of communities, some of them have increasingly of NGOs from developing their program strategic plans as they look shown reluctance to support customary overhead expenses (equipment, salaries and rent). In the process they have diverted attention for more funding to fill the gaps. This keeps them away from sticking to their own mission as most of them are usually not strategically ready to explore alternative sources. How can an NGO run a project effectively when a donor declines to support salaries for staff that are going to implement the project in the first place? With no salaries allocated, the project cannot attract the appropriate skills to implement; how can the project be effective in this way?

The number of indigenous NGOs in the developing world continues to increase and brings in an element of competition for financial resources since most NGOs chase funding from the same donors. This in turn gives the opportunity of choice for donors based on the level of quality of proposals among others. It is therefore not guaranteed that a request for funds will always receive a positive response.

Generally, funding for NGOs in the developing world is based on the time frames of the project cycle. If for instance the project life span is two years, there is pressure to deliver the targets within the stipulated time frame. If resources are not expended within that time frame, a few lucky ones will be granted a no cost extension while the rest have to surrender the remaining funds. The result sometimes is that the NGOs would rush to spend the money within the stipulated time frame and consequently compromise on quality in terms of processes and impact of the work done.

If you embark on a journey from one indigenous NGO to another to hear what their stories are on resource mobilization for their NGOs, you will likely end up with a pattern similarly highlighted in the next few paragraphs. In an encounter with Michael (not real name) he narrates that the fact that funding is tied to project time frames only, means more attention is paid to the project while the institution implementing the project is neglected. This is like paying attention to a passenger and his or her destination while neglecting the vehicle that carries them or like caring for the baby while neglecting the mother that carries it on the back.

Then Ken (not real name) shares his experiences during the time he presided over an indigenous NGO that almost collapsed during his tenure. He tackles the aspect of unpredictability on the part of donors which he sees as another element that presents challenges to NGOs in the developing world. Sometimes donors may change strategy, thematic areas of interest and even geographical coverage for a whole range of reasons. Such developments usually come in form of abrupt news to the affected NGOs.

Ken's NGO which is based in one of the Southern African countries had been responsible for facilitating land justice as part of the civil society initiatives on land issues and had been receiving funding from a British international NGO for over five years. The international NGO changed its strategy and decided to remove land issues as a priority thematic area. Consequently, it pulled out its support to the local NGO abruptly, at a critical time in terms of achievement of milestones for the land campaign. What happened in the end was that the local NGO became paralyzed financially and its campaign to push for enactment of the land bill and operationalization of the land policy fell on the wayside. Some staff went for seven months without pay.

Sometimes changes in governments in the west, where most NGOs in the developing world access their funding, can also change the whole dynamics of funding. Depending on the ideology of the governing parties, focus may change e.g. they may put more interest on domestic issues such as immigration trends or social welfare while others would focus more on different regions of the world. In 2010 the UK voters ushered in a new government under the Conservatives in coalition with the Liberal Democrats. Naturally a spending review for public funds was done, comprehensively in the midst of the global economic crisis.

Despite the cuts and reforms announced, the foreign aid budget was going to be protected and there would be an increase of 0.7% to the GNP. While this should potentially be good news for the developing world in general, the catch would be disappointing to the developing world as the government planned to link such spending more closely to its own national security strategy. In that case it meant availing more resources to countries viewed as terrorist hotspots such as Afghanistan, Iraq and Yemen.

Another aspect of the foreign aid strategy was that the UK government would focus on women in developing countries. In this respect the UK government was aiming at doubling the number of lives of women and babies saved through its aid by 2015. This case study of an election outcome and subsequent strategic changes on aid serves to illustrate the need for NGOs especially the indigenous ones from the developing world to be awake and aware of what is happening around the world. These events and trends tend to have some kind of (positive or negative) impact on their funding, and consequently on their thematic areas of interest. It can be deduced here that for the UK government, as of now, security and maternal health are its priority areas for foreign aid.

The environmental context itself is in a state of flux in terms of events and emergent patterns. This can also affect the manner and levels in which donors could avail resources to NGOs. Some events are natural for instance the Asian Tsunami of 2004 and the Haiti Earthquake of 2010 while others are manmade such as terrorist acts across the world. Natural disasters such as the Tsunami and the Haiti earthquake saw the immediate shift of world attention and television cameras. This in turn sparked a chain of reactions including more passionate donations from professional donors as well as private individuals especially from the western world. In such circumstances, ongoing NGO development projects supported by the donors in other parts of the developing world may suffer the shocks as well. Prioritization of resources in such circumstances would generally favor where there is urgency of need. Then there are general trends in terms of themes in fashion; currently climate change at global level and food security in the developing world are some of the trendy themes receiving attention from the major donors.

My journey continues with a visit to Doreen's (not real name) NGO where she is executive director. She laments about delayed disbursement of funding as another challenge that NGOs in the developing world have to put up with. While donors require timely submission of reports from the NGOs they are supporting, it is not uncommon that they do not meet the deadlines of disbursing the funds they committed. While the NGOs have to attach an explanatory note and apology for delayed submission of financial and/or progress reports, a good number of donors do not usually portray any sense of obligation to explain their delays in fund disbursement. The short of it is that the balance of power tilts towards the side that holds the purse.

Then I come across a letter to the editor published in one of the dailies. The letter is authored by one of the civil society activists commenting on another issue but its contents spill over to resource mobilization challenges. He insinuates that in a more subtle way sometimes NGOs in the developing world face the challenge of dealing with donors' in country grants or desk officers who pander to nepotism or outright corruption. For instance there have been instances where desk officers will primarily push through project proposals from NGOs headed by "home boys or girls" regardless of the quality of the proposal or the project's potential impact on society or specific constituency. In some cases grants officers may demand a "commission" for facilitating approval for a project.

Some donors generally place very strict conditions that are likely to suffocate emerging NGOs in the developing world. Such strict conditions may be placed across or on some points of the fundraising value chain. Mercy, a senior programme manager at her NGO shares the stress they went through to access funding from a certain multilateral western donor. She narrates that they went through very stringent scrutiny punctuated by a lot of paperwork over a period as long as a year prior to approval. Then upon approval, another strict condition was put in which the donor was to withhold 20% of the funding until the end of project report had been submitted. This meant the NGO had to risk its own financial resources to cover expenses amounting to 20% and hope that it would be refunded, something not guaranteed. This was also besides the demand that the NGO had to commit another 20% of the budget from its own resources as a contribution to the project. In reality, the NGO had to set aside 40% of the project budget from its other sources. This is a tall order from most indigenous NGOs in the developing world as their resource base is narrow and weak. This however illustrates the extent to which donors can go with their conditions. Other examples of conditions placed by donors include submission of project progress reports every month. In such circumstances, officers prioritize the reports at the expense of project activities on the ground. Documentation is both energy and time consuming and is an intellectual exercise. Naturally, extra attention is given to a document that is going to be submitted to a donor. This consumes a lot of time in the working week every month. Ironically the chances are that such numerous reports are not even read by those demanding them.

Sometimes donors want to dictate their own approach even if they are in agreement with the theme that an NGO is working on such as education or general livelihoods security. The poor and desperate NGO may accept the demand because it is a means to access funds from the donor, yet they may not have the necessary technical knowledge and skills to execute the approach. I once headed a development communication NGO which used the approach of direct radio based dialogue between rural communities and service providers. With time this attracted other players in the development communication arena and one donor approached and presented a financial offer if and only if we used radio drama for the project they were ready to support. While it was simple to listen to and may be simple to read here, the whole set up of radio drama requires different kind of skills, organization and resources. Strategically, our NGO was not ready for that though the financial incentive from a major donor from the west was inviting. We turned down the offer and this was possible because we were not in a desperate mode. Reflecting on this we notice that numerous NGOs from the developing world are subject to manipulation and eventually abandon their own missions and strategies because of pressure and desperation for money.

In extreme cases some donors have forced NGOs not work with any donor apart from themselves. Despite such commitments the donors have ended up giving short notices for discontinuation of funding, leaving such NGOs panicking while others have collapsed. Other donors also deploy less experienced expatriates from their home countries in the form of Technical Assistants (TAs) to oversee the projects they are funding. It is not uncommon to hear management of such NGOs whispering and murmuring their suspicions that such donors were in a ploy to creating jobs for homeboys and girls at the expense of the local NGOs staff

Implications

The scenarios described above have serious negative implications on the NGOs and the work that they do. To begin with, local NGOs with their narrow and weak financial base become very desperate for funding and will likely accept money even under strict conditions just to improve their liquidity. In the process the NGOs lose their autonomy as they cannot work according to their vision and mission. Their strategic plans become disposable luxuries in the thick of desperation. They literary are devoid of any bargaining power when dealing with donors. Local NGOs are suffocated and remain poorer than they were. Take the example of a donor demanding a contribution of 20% by the NGO and goes further to withhold another 20% from its contribution of 80% as "security for good performance"; the NGO is at risk of not getting the withheld 20% if in the opinion of the donor, the project has not had the impact it was intended to. Where would the poor NGO get such funds to make up for the 40% percent?

The impact of the local NGOs' work at the grassroots level is compromised as some of these conditions are administratively taxing. It is as if the project staff is working for the donors and not the communities on whose behalf they acquired the funding.

In their bid to keep the donors pleased, it becomes a necessary evil for some NGOs to engage in unethical behavior through cooking up certain data so that the reports win a nod rather than a wrinkle on the donor's forehead. By having made up figures, opportunities for learning from the experiences in field are lost by the donor, the NGO and the wider community of development practice.

Cases of donors dictating to NGOs which districts, zones or provinces to implement projects supported by their funds are not strange either. Some NGOs with brilliant project proposals earmarked for initiatives in certain geographical areas have ended up being swayed to work in areas of the donors' choices because of the need to secure the funding they desperately need.

The game of power is evident here and it is clear as to who has an edge over the other and why. Complete reliance on aid money comes with a lot more risks than what NGOs may imagine. Sometimes donors may delay in approving the funds and the NGOs cannot run effectively during the period they are awaiting approval. A few lucky ones may get what is called "bridge funding" as they await the final decisions.

The above scenario can be summarized as follows:

- Donors' behavior is unpredictable
- Heavy reliance on a single donor is potentially catastrophic
- Conditions set out by donors may undermine the autonomy of NGO and its purpose
- There is bias towards projects neglecting the organizations that implement them

Under these circumstances most NGOs find themselves in a tight corner. It should be stated however that it is not in all cases that donors place stringent conditions and also that it is not necessarily bad to have the conditions attached to funding. This helps in enhancing accountability considering that cases of abuse are not uncommon.

Chapter Two

Resource Mobilization Planning

This chapter focuses on important insights for NGOs when they are embarking on resource mobilization planning processes. The discussion is meant to raise awareness that effective resource mobilization does not happen to NGOs but rather it is the NGOs that should happen to effective resource mobilization. The chapter further introduces revenue generation ideas that may appear nontraditional to leadership in most indigenous NGOs, however, they have been tried and tested and proven to work in a diversity of contexts across the globe. Success case studies have been presented to provide inspiration to all indigenous NGOs that aspire to attain financial sustainability and the consequent autonomy. They are applicable to the indigenous NGOs in the developing world just as they are to the western bred international NGOs.

This chapter further shares tips on practical steps for acquiring information about donors, how to read your environment and make sense out of it in relation to resource mobilization, examining internal capacities and how to develop a budget for a project proposal among others. This should be the transformational chapter for you as far as resource mobilization is concerned.

First we should examine the intrinsic nature of funds raised from donors and funds raised from non-traditional sources.

Restricted and unrestricted funds

When donors give money to a non-for-profit NGO, they normally place restrictions as to what this money can be used for. Restricted funds are those that come with terms and conditions about what the funds may or may not be used for, usually secured from donors. For instance if your NGO received funds for a project under a budget that did not provide for purchase of a computer, you may not procure one using those funds even in the event that a computer has been stolen or broken down beyond repair despite that such a computer were useful for the attainment of the project objectives. Unrestricted funds are those that usually come from alternative sources and their usage is left to the discretion of the decisions by the NGO. The understanding though is that the discretionary usage is within the framework of attaining organizational goals. The more unrestricted funds an NGO has the higher the level of its autonomy and the higher the more restricted funds, the higher its dependency on donors. Some discussion on usage of unrestricted funds has been advanced in chapter four.

How then can NGOs start working on this? First is to acknowledge that donor organizations are established to make available financial resources to alleviate suffering, improve quality of life for and empower vulnerable populations. Since money from donors will be available for that purpose, opportunities have to be created and seized by the NGOs in the developing world.

Most NGOs examined during the research on this book cited overhead expenses as the major challenge that donors are reluctant to support adequately as NGOs may need. This could be a good starting point to explore the potential to develop resource mobilization plan.

Donor dependency ratio

An NGO needs to assess what its donor dependency ratio is as this gives a picture of the state of its financial autonomy. The parameters of donor dependency and financial autonomy are placed in polar positions as can be noted from the figure below adapted from Mango (2005).

100% Donor dependent	*Where are you?*	100% Self- financing

To be able to determine where your organization is, the formula below (also from Mango, 2005) can be used. Calculate how much the annual total income is and how much of that is from donors. The figures are

20

placed correspondingly in the formula to calculate donor dependency as a percentage.

$$\frac{\text{Total Donor Income} \times 100}{\text{Total Income}}$$

If your organization gets all its income from donors, it means its donor dependency is 100% and vice-versa. Most organizations have a donor dependency averaging 90%. BRAC is in a class of its own at 27%.

Planning Ahead

The NGO then has to set targets over any period of years in terms of planned annual budgets and level of autonomy it plans to achieve. The table below illustrates this using a two year and five year time frame with the neutral currency called the NC.

Table 1 Financial sustainability targets

Current annual budget	Targeted annual total income in two years' time	Targeted annual total income in five years' time
NC 500,000	NC 700,000	NC 1,000,000
Current annual income from donors	**Targeted annual income from donors in two years' time**	**Targeted annual income from donors in five years' time**
NC 450,000	NC 560,000	NC 600,000
Current annual self-generated revenue	**Targeted annual self-generated revenue in two years' time**	**Targeted annual self-generated revenue in five years' time**
NC 50,000	NC 140,000	NC 400,000
Current donor dependence ratio	**Targeted donor dependence ratio in two years' time**	**Targeted donor dependence ratio in five years' time**
90%	80%	60%

This table demonstrates that this NGO plans to reduce its donor dependency from 90% to 60% over a period of five years while at the same time it plans to increase its overall annual income by 100% over the same period. However, with increasing contribution from own income sources, rate of increase in funding from donors will have reduced.

Planning for resource mobilization from donors

After developing the targets, the organization should then facilitate a team brainstorming session to generate project ideas based on its vision and mission. However, it is important that when it comes to project conceptualization, NGO leadership should understand the models programme based and project based fundraising. The discussion on these two models has been ably guided by the framework adapted from Mango's (2005) funding types' matrix.

Project based and programme based models for fundraising

The income generated in project based funding is usually restricted and it is also short-term in nature. This is generally from institutional donor agencies. Such funding is project-specific, and on average would last for 1-3 years. There is no assurance for extension and as such the project impact may not be achieved adequately while at the same time the NGOs' access to the funding ends once the stated project period expires. Unfortunately this is the most common form of financing for indigenous NGOs in the developing world..

Programme- based funding is a long term arrangement but still comes with restrictions just as in project funding. In this arrangement the donor provides funds to the NGOs based on broader programme themes and not specific projects. Such arrangements for long term funding are usually possible after establishing a strong working relationship with a donor. This type of funding, in my view, provides a safety net in some respects because there is commitment for funds for a long time by the donor. This, however, does not take away the possibility of donors pulling away earlier should they decide to do so due to various reasons. These may range from change of priorities, reduced budgets caused by global events like the recent economic crisis or by new or existing government policy in the case of bilateral donors such as USAID and DFID among others. In some cases extreme restrictions have been placed on indigenous NGOs receiving programme funding. Examples of such restrictions include not allowing the NGOs to engage any other donor during the period they are funding the organization as observed by Malunga (2007) cited in Kapyepye (2009).

Having looked at the two different models of resource mobilization from donors, let us discuss potential projects that can be implemented by indigenous NGOs in the developing world. This is where strategic planning becomes an important resource as it provides the broad framework from which project ideas can be generated. It gives the direction the organization should take over a period of time and as such project ideas should be drawn from it.

Below is a table from one real session conducted with an NGO called Friends of AIDS Support Trust (FAST) from Malawi in 2009.

Table 2 Project ideas for donor funding in a resource mobilization plan

Project idea	Potential sources of funding
Nutrition/ Livelihoods project	To be researched
Early Childhood Care Project	UNICEF To be researched , SAT Stars Foundation
Bursary Scheme for Secondary school Education	Chell foundation SLF Raising Malawi Trust
Grandmothers Project	Stephen Lewis Foundation
Group therapy Project	SAT
Childs Right project	UNICEF Stars Foundation
Life skills development for the youth	To be researched

The strategic objectives in the strategic plan and/or the projects being proposed and agreed upon can then be used to determine the programme areas if the project wants to embark on the programme based funding model.

Planning for resource mobilization from non-traditional sources – a social enterprise model

The next few sections tackle a business approach in generating revenue for a non-for-profit organization. This concept is called social enterprising and reflects a departure from the norm as far as fundraising is concerned among most indigenous NGOs in the developing world. **A social enterprise** is defined as a *commercial business venture operated by an NGO with a social aim.* Social enterprise projects are aimed at empowering NGOs to operate income generating activities and to make a social impact i.e. to fulfill the mission of the NGO.

There is a common belief that because NGOs are not-for-profit, they cannot engage in commercial activities. This is not correct. What differentiates a not-for-profit organization engaging in commercial activity from a private sector company is the purpose of usage of the revenue generated. While a private sector company will distribute part of surplus income (profit) to its shareholders or owners for their own private or personal use, a not-for-profit organization will use its surplus to meet its programme and/or administrative expenses or any other use that is furthering its social objectives.

The next item should be to brainstorm ideas can be generated on potential sources of own revenue. Being a brainstorming session, ideas should be allowed to flow from all members first and then to be refined later. However, it is important before proceeding to examine the terms *General Fundraising and Core Financing,* as they are helpful in understanding categorization of activities for self-income generation.

General fundraising and core financing

General fundraising involves short-term funding and the funds raised in this way are unrestricted in nature. The funds can be raised through one-off fundraising activities and donations from the public. It is helpful when the organisation wants to build up reserves or fill a short term gap arising from instances where a project funding agreement has failed to cover 100% of the implementation costs.

Whereas in core financing, the income comes from enterprise activities by way of goods or services or both. Such funding is more reliable, regular and flexible; and can be used for the NGOs' core operations and even programme or project funding as is the case with BRAC. This is a higher level of organizational funding which requires competences not currently viewed as crucial in most indigenous NGOs in the developing world. This brings a more disciplined entrepreneurial culture within the framework of a not-for-profit institution. This is what should mark the departure in terms of existing mental models on enterprise based thinking among the NGO leadership i.e. management and boards.

Having examined the terms *general fundraising and core financing*, the brainstorming session can then be done. Where resources permit or negotiation is possible for a volunteer, a business development expert can be invited to assist in the refining of the ideas.

Table 3 Project ideas for social enterprises in a resource mobilization plan

Proposed IGA	by when	Resources we have	Resources we need	Skills required	Responsible persons	Budget Estimate
Business centre (Internet café, training centre, photocopying and printing)	Dec 2010	Space Internet Connection	Finances Computers Photocopier (heavy duty) Printer Furniture Stationery Other consumables	Secretarial skills Software & hardware Maintenance skills Security Cleaner	IGA Officer and Business Centre administrator	
Guest house	Dec 2012	Land	Building Structure Furniture Building materials Finances	House keeping, hospitality skills, housekeeping Skills, food production	IGA Officer Guest House Admin	
Livestock project (Poultry and Piggery)	Dec 2010	Land	Finances Khola Seed stock especially pigs Layers Feed	Animal husbandry skills Security	IGA Officer	
Paraffin pump	Dec 2011	Land	Finances Pump tank and supporting infrastructure	Book keeping skills Security	IGA Officer	
Conference hall	In progress	3 halls (one in use)	Hall at head office needs upgrading e.g. furniture and accessories Two site office halls require materials for completion of construction and sanitation facilities and water supply	Conference management And house keeping skill	IGA Officer and Conference Administration	

The table above reflects the raw thinking of one indigenous NGO in the developing world which decided to take a conscious and more structured step towards an entrepreneurial approach to resource mobilization and running of affairs. This is in itself a major form of policy change and requires new ways of thinking and acting transcending various strata of the organization. Policy change in this instance means the boards of NGOs in the developing world must be the change drivers and live up to the challenge since these changes are intrinsically matters of policy at high level. In our research, it was discovered that in most cases NGO boards were inactive in general and more prominently when it comes to resource mobilization. The standard acceptable practice in organizational governance is that decisions and guidance on resource mobilization are the responsibility of boards as such decisions border on policy.

Embracing the culture of social enterprise in NGOs

One of the fundamental challenges NGOs taking a business approach will have to face is their institutional set up. By embracing an enterprise approach to resource mobilization, indigenous NGOs in the developing world should brace for a cultural change in the manner they run their affairs. There is some balancing act that has to take place in terms of institutional set up if social enterprise is to succeed. There are several models that are being applied as far as integration of business enterprises in NGOs is concerned. Below three scenarios are discussed.

Running enterprises within the existing NGO institutional set up

During the research, it was found that most of those NGOs that had attempted generating their own income had embarked on some brilliant ideas ranging from running tree nurseries and rearing of livestock to full scale desk top publishing. However, in most of these cases, there were no deliberate strategies on how to harness the business enterprises or how to use the income they raised from there. Management of such enterprises was just like running any department in the NGOs without due consideration of the fact that this was pursuing a different line of service which required a different approach to running it. While in some cases there were dedicated staff implementing commercial activities, management generally remained under the direct control of executive directors. Generally executive directors in NGOs are busy and tuned to raising funds through requests to donors. While direct oversight keeps the directors updated on the day to day operations, they usually do not possess specialized skills in running business enterprises at professional level. In one case,

28

an NGO raising up to 15% of its income from desktop publishing was still facing serious financial shortfalls and yet this publishing unit was being underutilized, the staff were de-motivated and never received support in terms of marketing the services they offered.

In another case, a youth NGO was very creative again with its enterprising ideas running a youth centre with a conference hall, a computer resource centre and a restaurant among others. Although it was able to raise 5% of its total income from these enterprises and keep them in good shape, there was still a lot of promise to be realized from the investment. However the absence of a dedicated unit to oversee all its enterprises which also included a guest house meant that business development lacked the necessary attention to grow these enterprises to another level.

It is not advisable therefore, for NGOs to run business enterprises under the regular set ups that they have had prior to running the commercial entities. While it is understandable that at the beginning of such projects it may not be necessary or easy to set up dedicated entities, it should not be overlooked or ignored as the business enterprises get more established.

Establishing a dedicated department

Establishing a business enterprise department to focus on the commercial activities of the organisation is one of the routes that an NGO needs to take. This will ensure that personnel and resources are focused on their work. The lines are clear between business activities and social services provided under the different thematic areas. The advantage with this option is that in most legal jurisdictions it does not require statutory legal processes for registration of the businesses as separate entities since they fall within an already existing legal entity. It will also be easier to seek "kindhearted" support from fellow NGOs if the business enterprises have an NGO identity. Another advantage is that this department can also take on all resource mobilization responsibilities for the NGO i.e. combining donor relations and business development and management. The challenge with the option may be the management of the balance between social and commercial identities.

Establishing a separate company

The third option is for the NGO to establish a separate legal entity as a commercial subsidiary focusing on enterprise development with its own articles of association. This company would then be providing support for core funding as is the case mostly or going further to support programme or project activities as is the case with BRAC. The advantage with this is that each entity would have its own management and there would be no question of divided attention while the commercial entity is ultimately accountable to the NGO. Subject to legal jurisdictions, the governance models for such entities may differ. For instance the Indonesian law restricts board members of NGOs from sitting on the boards of the commercial entities they set up; neither can they play any other direct role in the commercial entity. The option of setting up a separate commercial entity is a more demanding strategic management process that requires even greater management discipline but is potentially more rewarding. Commercial entities need not be too sophisticated though.

In all the three scenarios looked at above, it is very important for NGOs to remain focused on their mission and not get carried away with any financial successes generated by the business venture. This comes with organizational discipline, and leadership has an important role of safeguarding the focus.

Partnerships with the private sector

NGOs in the developing world have not generally come to the realization that they could strategically harness sound partnerships with the private sector. There is the strong tendency among NGOs of looking at the corporate world as capitalist schemers who are only interested in profiteering and exploiting workers and consumers. While some commercial players rightly deserve the accusations, the NGO sector itself cannot claim to be devoid of such collective guilt; moreover these persistent negative thoughts have blinded the NGOs from seeing the sunny side of partnering with the private sector in a manner that is sustainable and benefits the NGOs themselves, their beneficiaries and the corporate world. There is no single player, be it in the public sector, civil society or private sector that has an all-embracing know-how and resources to deal with the complex social problems and as diverse as they are. Rein et al (2005) citing ODI/IBLF (2004) describe partnerships as follows:

> …unlike contractual relationships…they seek not to shift responsibility and risk from one party to another, but to share risks, pool resources and talents and deliver mutual benefits for each party.

Case studies on effective partnerships between NGOs and the private sector

Below are case studies of how effective dialogue between NGOs and the private sector can bring about strategic partnerships.

TACDRUP, Dolefil and PhilRice from Philippines[1]

In the Philippines, a local farmers' advocacy organization called TACDRUP entered into a partnership with Dolefil, a subsidiary of Dole Food Company, a private sector player. TACDRUP is a Philippine-based non-profit foundation put up by a group of social development workers in June 1980. As one of the pioneering social development non-government organizations in Southern Philippines, TACDRUP committed to pursue structural change and to facilitate the laying down of a mechanism for people's active participation in sustainable development and responsible governance. One of TACDRUP's two major themes is food security and environmental protection. The government agency responsible for rice production, Philippine Rice Research Institute (PhilRice) was also brought in to play a supportive role on the rice value chain. They had to come together to produce rice of sufficient quality for a Japanese market that appeared to be a challenge because of its choosy behavior. This partnership achieves the distinct goals for each party in the partnership. PhilRice as a government agency has the goal of

---

[1] Adapted from Steve Waddell's article Core Competences, A Key Force in Business-Government-Civil Society Collaborations

improved rice productivity. Rice is a major crop in the Philippines and its impact on livelihoods cannot be ignored. On the other hand Dolefil's goal as a commercial player is that of making profits while TACDRUP aims at attaining social and environmental benefits for smaller farmers.

In this relationship, PhilRice produces quality rice seeds while TACDRUP facilitates farmers' credit access, provides training, processing and packaging. Dolefil buys seeds and the rice produced at a guaranteed floor price. Profits are shared between Dolefil and TACDRUP on an equal basis. From this partnership we can see that Dolefil as a private sector player has a role to play on the value chain of rice and in the process, TACDRUP is able to fulfill its objectives in advocating for famers' rights.

Youth Network and Counseling (YONECO) and TNM Limited in Malawi

Youth Network and Counseling (YONECO), established in September 1997 is a Malawian NGO which exists to contribute to the creation of a self-reliant HIV/AIDS free society that respects democratic values and principles. It got registered under Malawi's Trustees Incorporation Act in 1999. YONECO is committed to empowering youth, women and children, preventing the spread of HIV infection, mitigating the impact of AIDS and promoting democracy and human rights for socioeconomic development. TNM is a telecommunications company providing mobile phone services in Malawi. Established in 1995, TNM is a wholly Malawian owned company and is listed on the Malawi Stock Exchange (MSE).

YONECO and TNM have a formal partnership agreement in which YONECO can identify a potential area of need in the area of youth, women and children welfare and submit proposals for consideration by TNM. The same applies to TNM that it can identify a need and request YONECO to develop an intervention in support of youth, women and children. TNM has committed to partner with YONECO in the long term but the initial partnership agreement was for three years from 2008 to 2011.

One of the initiatives through which the partnership has been implemented is the *Tithandizane* Helpline, a toll free facility through which youth and women in difficult circumstances such as domestic abuse, can reach YONECO to report and also seek counseling. TNM has also provided a short messaging bulk tool solution to support the YONECO helpline and other initiatives requiring the use of SMS besides refurbishment of the YONECO drop-in centers and safe places located in several parts of Malawi. The cost of maintaining the helpline was estimated at roughly US$350 per month while the refurbishment of the drop-in centers was estimated at US$32,000. The costs for the other project initiatives would be based on the needs arising.

Through the partnership, YONECO has accessed telecommunication equipment which has also been maintained and whose services covered by TNM while the NGO has been able to contribute to the fulfillment of its mission of empowering youth, women and children. On the other hand, TNM has fulfilled part of its social obligations to the vulnerable target groups by tapping on already existing expertise at YONECO. TNM is able to focus its expertise on their core business of a mobile phone service provider while it is able to attain its social responsibility with external expertise.

RASA and AMANCO in Mexico[2]

RASA (Red de Agricultores Sustenables or the Sustainable Farmers Network) is an NGO helping small farmers located in poor regions of Guerrero State in Mexico; attain higher living standards under a framework of participatory democracy and social responsibility. RASA was legally constituted in 1993 but had over 25 years of experience in rural projects, providing farmers with commercial and manufacturing rural services, as well as specialized advisory and training. Amanco on the other hand is a subsidiary company of GrupoNueva, private sector player, which spearheads the production and marketing of water management systems in Latin America with a focus on the building sector and on drip-feed irrigation for agriculture.

[2] Source: Growing Inclusive Markets

For decades, small farmers in Latin America have faced low productivity, inefficiency and unfair prices due to the prevalence of commercial intermediaries. Against this backdrop, Amanco developed a hybrid value chain model for serving this low-income market. As part of its endeavour, first in Guatemala where it worked with the NGO Opción and then in Mexico, the company experienced a shift from selling water conveyance supplies to offering integrated irrigation solutions. Amanco partnered with RASA, an NGO that traditionally worked with small farmers in Guerrero. RASA's decision to partner with Amanco was part of a broader strategy to contribute to the rehabilitation of the lemon sector in Guerrero in a context of a production shortage in the local markets.

The community selected for the pilot project was La Testaruda, with which RASA was already working. The pilot project was initiated in 2005. This community was comprised by a total of 52 small lemon farmers, who on average owned two hectares of land. Living conditions in this community were of high deprivation. In terms of farming activities, low-income lemon producers were subject to low levels of productivity due to the old age of their plants, the prevalence of archaic irrigation methods, the need for modern equipment and the lack of capital to invest in it. Small farmers had access to groundwater, mainly through wells and boreholes, because there was no piped water service. Water inefficiencies were common, since traditional irrigation methods implied manual irrigation with a hose for two or three hours until the available water deposits emptied. Under those circumstances only farmers with adequate water availability were able to produce enough to make a living. Those without access to traditional water sources depended on the rainy seasons. Farmers from La Testaruda sold their lemons in the local markets and nearest cities without being able to reach larger wholesalers or supermarket chains. Agriculture involved the whole family with siblings and wives traditionally supporting with the farm duties.

Through this partnership the Amanco was able to serve groups of farmers, rather than individual farmers. Besides acting as a distributor and promoter for the company, RASA provided additional services such as technical assistance, facilitated access to financing and commercialization channels, as well as the administrative procedures for getting public subsidies. In exchange for the services provided to low-income clients, RASA received a 20 percent commission plus free training from Amanco. RASA assets were its community closeness and knowledge, its familiarity with the region and its problems, as well as the trust and legitimacy it had among its network of contacts.

The installation of new irrigation systems represented reductions in labour costs or time devoted to irrigation. What required from three to four days under manual irrigation schemes could be done automatically, freeing up small farmers' time for other farm and personal duties.

Amanco's irrigation systems made a more efficient use of water possible. There were different percentages of water savings, depending on the irrigation system used, with a maximum of 60 percent. Besides the rationalization of the use of water, the new irrigation systems helped to halt soil erosion.

The great level of organization and coordination among small scale farmers yielded the most positive results. Because of their association, they realized that there was a huge difference between the real market prices and those paid to them by commercial intermediaries: while the intermediary paid them two pesos per crate (from 22 to 25 kilos), in the market the price was up to 13, which is 6.5 times higher.

Some key lessons from case studies on NGO-Private Sector Partnerships

There is mutual benefit from partnerships between NGOs and the private sector. Through such partnerships, NGOs can tap on the financial or other benefits to facilitate delivery of their core business of serving the needy and vulnerable. At the same time the private sector is able to focus on its own core business while availing resources and tapping into the NGOs' expertise to facilitate fulfillment of its corporate social obligations.

Environmental scanning for resource mobilization using PEST or PESTEL analysis

Since the NGOs are operating in a dynamic environment, it is important that they examine carefully the context in which they are operating. They need to understand the events and trends emerging in order to surmise the implications of such on their resource mobilization drive. One such tool used to scan the environment is called PEST analysis which also has an extended derivative called PESTEL. The acronym stands for Political, Economic, Societal, Technological, Environmental and Legislative. The latter version is in fashion now due to the increasing attention on environmental issues globally.

Trends and events can be examined at three levels namely Global, Regional and National. In this case regional level is used to describe continents or sub-continents whichever is applicable in your case (Asia, South East Asia, Africa, Sub-Saharan Africa, Middle East, Latin America, Caribbean etc). It is important that a PESTEL analysis is conducted at all levels so that linkages can be made and implications deduced on what they mean to the organization in as far as resource mobilization is concerned. The template below can be used to guide the process of conducting a PESTEL analysis.

36

Table 4 PESTEL analysis template

Global Level	
Political	**Economic**
Social	**Technological**
Environmental	**Legislative**
Regional Level	
Political	**Economic**
Social	**Technological**
Environmental	**Legislative**
National Level	
Political	**Economic**
Social	**Technological**
Environmental	**Legislative**

The key question here is; *What implications does this have for our resource mobilization drive?*

Assessing internal capacity for resource mobilization using SWOT analysis

Having examined the external environment, the organization is supposed to examine its internal environment by examining its capabilities at various levels e.g. physical and financial resources, skills and competences, systems and structure, vision, mission and strategy among others. Using a framework called SWOT analysis. SWOT stands for Strengths, Weaknesses, Opportunities and Threats. The first two parameters focus on the internal capabilities while the last two focus on the external environment. In a way, opportunities and threats overlap with PESTEL analysis and as such can be used for triangulation and confirmation of your organizations environmental scan. The table below could be a useful template when you are conducting a SWOT analysis.

Table 5 SWOT analysis template

Strengths	Weaknesses
Opportunities	Threats

Once again you also make deductions of the SWOT as to what it implies to your resource mobilization drive by asking the same question: *What implications does this have for our resource mobilization drive?*

When you are complete with your PESTEL and SWOT analyses, you have a good picture of what you need to maximize on that is already working well and what you need to work on that is not working well at the moment. You also get a heightened level of consciousness of what your environment means to your organization at any given time. This experience should be understood as a process rather than an event. Leadership in most NGOs in the developing world faces the challenge of taking all this resource mobilization planning and the newly acquired knowledge as an event and with time it fades away from their agenda during implementation.

This is why regular reviews of plans like these are useful so that the fire keeps burning.

Establishing contacts with donors

Establishing contact with donors can be done through various avenues and the key point is to keep eyes and ears wide open at any given time. The following are examples of ways in which contacts with donors can be established:

Publications: These publications include newspapers, newsletters, annual reports and brochures among others. For instance, information about donors can be acquired from newspapers in a variety of ways that you probably often overlook because you have not put your mind into a fundraising mode. Some donors place adverts in newspapers calling for proposals. This is a more obvious way that could lead you into contacting a donor. Other ways include articles on some story which may mention the donor in passing or as the main subject of the news. The most important thing is to look at news contents in such publications beyond the surface. Consider this scenario which marked a turning point in the life of one NGO with which the author had some association ten years ago. *A funding agency had put up an advert for a vacancy of a Human Rights Programme Officer. Up to this point, the NGO leadership had no prior knowledge that the funding agency had recently introduced a human rights component. The advert prompted leadership to establish initial contact with the funding agency to understand their areas of interest in human rights funding. This contact led to a long term funding partnership which had continued for nine years at the time of writing this book and it was still strong.*

Almost all donors produce annual reports and such documents can also provide useful information about donors to enable NGOs take necessary steps.

Forums and networks: Through affiliation to networks, NGOs have an opportunity to learn of existing opportunities for funding in their sector. Sharing of information through attending meetings or through general network communication, NGOs stand a chance of getting to know donors that can support their work and it is up to them to take it up further with the donors. Sometimes donors are invited to such network meetings and the strategic fundraisers can take advantage of the donors' presence to establish initial contacts. This is why it is important that NGOs build a good image for themselves even through their personnel. There is a tendency sometimes among indigenous NGOs to send to meetings uninformed representatives who do not provide any strategic leverage.

Informal encounters: When you have trained your mind to be in the fundraising mode, you can create and seize opportunities in the most unlikely circumstances. With appropriate social interaction skills, you can get in touch with donors' representatives at any occasion such as cocktail parties or other functions organized by government, NGOs or the private sector. Informal encounters can even take place on a flight and you have a chance to initiate preliminary dialogue or necessary tips to win funding for your organization. Again the issue of image is important. This is the time to exchange business cards! Even the way your business cards are designed speaks volumes about your organization.

Internet search: The internet has become a must have item as it keeps growing in stature, what with the convergence of various forms of Information and Communication Technologies such as mobile phones? While some indigenous NGOs in the developing world may still be having challenges in terms of access, Internet penetration has greatly improved in recent years and it provides an opportunity for fundraising. By going on the search engines such as Google, one can get a treasure trove of information on donors across the globe and their areas of interest. Most donors have websites and that would direct a fundraiser to more focused information to enable them decide whether they should make contact or not. Some donors place their RFPs (Requests for Proposals) on their websites. In my conversation with an

Executive Director of an NGO, she narrated to me how they established contact with a donor they had not known before searching on the internet and how much interest their project proposal attracted interest to the extent that the negotiations ended up increasing the duration of the project from one year to three years!

Social media such as Facebook, Twitter and YouTube have also become an avenue for non-profit organizations to discover information about funders. Social media provide an informal platform where serious business between non-profit organizations and funders can cultivate serious business. It is the responsibility of the non-profit organizations to be proactive and make the first move.

Radio and television: Radio and television are media that appear unlikely to offer you ammunition for fundraising if you look at them with an ordinary eye. For instance, quite often stations such as the BBC or Etv News, CNN or Al Jazeera run documentaries on projects taking place across the globe and they would normally as part of narration, mention the funders of such interesting initiatives. Sometimes it is just a news story in a normal bulletin and somehow a donor or donors get mentioned. It is encounters like these that can lead your organization to a successful funding partnership if well harnessed.

Examining information about prospective donors

When embarking on resource mobilization through donor funding, the NGO must know very well the donors they will be approaching. You cannot just approach a donor with a project proposal before you get certain basics right. The following are some of the most fundamental factors that an NGO must explore on donors before committing time to develop project proposals:

Geographical factors: Some donors are specific in terms of the regions of the world they can support e.g. Caribbean, Sub-Saharan Africa, Asia etc. If your area of programme delivery work does not fall within that geographical scope, it is of no use to start engaging them for possible funding.

Socioeconomic factors: Get to understand which thematic areas the donors you have identified are supporting. Some have permanent interests in certain themes while others especially bilateral donors review regularly such themes to match with emerging policy interests of their governments. Themes may include empowerment of women or supporting water and sanitation or education. Depending on the themes of interest, you can explore which ones are within you areas of interest. For instance some donors with interest in women empowerment may accommodate a broad range of sub themes such as HIV & AIDS, education, microfinance or food security. Others would be very specific with subthemes e.g. scholarships to the girl child etc.

Funding cycles: Some donors can accept proposals any time while others have specific periods when they call for proposals and you need to be aware of the donors you are contacting have such mechanism in place. Some accept proposals on three month or six month cycles and you have to time your submission in line with the stated deadlines.

Other information on donors: Make sure that you understand the normal practices of particular donors to determine whether that would promote or antagonize your own interests. Know what their giving history is and whether their level of flexibility or inflexibility is. You may get to know this through other NGO beneficiaries in your country or from other countries. Some practices are informal and subtle but could have serious effects on your organization.

The role of documentation in marketing and resource mobilization

Record keeping is an important discipline for any organization that minds about posterity. It is such a great contributor to the sustainability of an organization that leadership cannot ignore. Indigenous NGOs in the developing world have big weakness in this area and that contributes to their inability to grow. Let us look at some of significant benefits that accrue from record keeping:

Credibility: when records are well managed, the NGO attains credibility among its stakeholders including donors. When others ask of information about your organization and you are able to retrieve and avail it promptly, it reflects your level of ability to get organized. That feeds into your credibility profile in the eyes of those you interact with. For instance if a prospective donor asks for a financial report or an evaluation report for a particular project and you cannot trace it, it is like failing to prove your suitability as a suitor in the presence of a prospective bride.

Learning and knowledge management: When an NGO documents and keeps a good account of what it is doing or has done on the ground, it provides a forum for its own learning and that of the outside world. Documented experiences are basis for new knowledge on certain aspects of development. A significant number of NGOs in the developing world have done some wonderful work in facilitating improvement of lives among disadvantaged groups but they cannot showcase it to the rest of the world to learn from and generate new knowledge because of poor documentation practices. When you cannot document and show the world what difference your work is making, you lose a great marking tool during resource mobilization. Donors are happy providing funding where there is evidence of a track record because the risk of the funding is deemed lower in that case.

Planning for the future: when your records are in good order, you are able to retrieve them without effort and you can easily make plans backed by documented reference points of the past. You have proper guidance for your plans when you have well maintained records. You do not have to reinvent the wheel each time you are planning.

Examples of records discussed above include reports of past and present projects, financial records, personnel records, constitution for the organization, annual reports; baseline study reports pictures; case studies of success stories among others. Five years ago I was contracted to conduct an evaluation of a project funded by one of the multilateral donors. As part of the literature review, my team and I needed to look at the baseline study report so that we could ably draw parallels between what was there before and then. After two years of project implementation, no one could trace the baseline report in the organization. This reflects badly on such an organization because, the evaluation was affected to significant extent in as far as objective analysis was concerned since benchmarking was absent. This is how indigenous NGOs take marks of their grades in the presence of donors. This helps them rationalize their perceptions towards indigenous NGOs as lacking capacity to do serious business on a larger scale budgets with bigger budgets.

Values and ethics in fundraising

Having looked at the planning processes for resource mobilization using a business model, it is necessary that we also look at issues of an NGO's core values and how they relate with each other. Organizational values are developed based on several factors among which the key ones are the sector in which the NGO is operating and the background of the organization. Values themselves cover various themes and this is also brings up the ethical dimension to bear.

An NGO that promotes child rights and welfare is likely to have key values that center on values along that line in their organizational practices. For example, a prospective employee with a record of child molestation would be of greater concern to a child rights NGO than would be to an environmental NGO. In the same way, resource mobilization practices for NGOs should not overlook this aspect because the NGOs are primarily driven by their core purpose which is also reflected in their values and the way they raise funds from donors or through commercial activity should not antagonize their mission. Some NGOs are faith-based and their drive for resource mobilization may also be affected because of the faith doctrine they pursue; for instance most faith organizations may not be in a position to partner with a cigarette manufacturing company. However, a child rights organization may partner with a cocoa growing company on an initiative aimed at eliminating child labor in the cocoa farms and other points on the cocoa value chain. An environmental NGO may partner with a mining company on a venture aimed at sustainable management of the environment while anti-mining NGOs may not consider that route at all because it goes against their values. The same applies to dealing with mainstream funding organizations some of whom also clearly state which types of organizations they would not with for instance some donors say they can only fund faith based or secular organizations only.

The underlying issue is that in your resource mobilization drive; make sure your core values are not undermined.

Ethical considerations are central in an NGO's quest for financial autonomy and strong balance needs to be attained. This ensures that it is able to champion its core values in its economic activities just as it does in its social activities. In the case of AYISE, as a youth focused organization, business ventures such as running a pub may not be applicable as this contradicts one of the foundation stones on which the organization was established i.e. to keep youth away from drug and alcohol abuse.

Budgeting in project proposals

Development of project proposals is a subject that is well tackled and addressed in other publications despite the continued gaps in practice among NGOs in the developing world. One of the major components of project proposal writing is the budget. Contrary to popular belief that budgeting is difficult and requires a sophisticated accounting procedure or genius, it just requires fiscal discipline. It is also important to take note that team work always has a greater chance of producing better results...remember the saying *two heads are better than one*. A project budget is not just about figures; and organizations should never make the mistake of leaving the preparation of figures to finance people alone. A project budget should be reflective of effective interdepartmental coordination of the organization. Figures themselves as prepared by finance do not mean anything unless they are given perspective by those responsible for implementation. That level of coordination ensures that calculations are done as accurately as possible and that the figures are corresponding to the activities. Assemble your team i.e. program staff, finance staff, admin staff to the budgeting process. Do not underestimate those that may not be directly involved in project implementation; remember that the projects in your organization do not operate as islands within the programs portfolio. For instance when you are dealing with stationery purchases for your projects, administrative staff are highly involved and they have a better practical feel of that area, as such their input into the budget should not be ignored.

A good starting point is to list all the activities and resources required to implement the proposed project. Your technical proposal which you will have developed already by this time becomes an important resource for this information. These activities and resources may be grouped by headings. There are different ways in which grouping of activities and resources is done and that depends on your style and also the requirements of the donor (if they have a particular format – some donors do not mind this).

A practical budgeting exercise

A heading like ***Project Communication*** may cover items such as *phone expenses, internet bills, and courier among* related expenses. It may even cover purchase, installation and maintenance of communication accessories. When you have grouped your items like this, you then start costing them.

Let's look at internet bills first. You may estimate that this project will contribute 25% of the monthly or quarterly expenses incurred by the whole organisation. If your total monthly internet bill is NC 2,500 you will then peg the monthly budget for this project at NC 2,500 x 0.25 which will give you NC 625 per month.

If your monthly phone bill is estimated at NC 12,000, your project budget per month would be NC 12,000 x 0.25 which translates into NC 3,000.

If average courier costs NC 1000 per parcel, you have to estimate the level of your outgoing parcel traffic that may arise from project transactions. Let us say you expect an average of 3 parcels every month; this means your courier expenses per month will be estimated at NC 1000 x 3 which is NC 3,000

Based on your experiences you may also determine the frequency at which communication installations are maintained. Let us say every six months at the estimated cost of NC 5000. If your records are up to date, this information should be easy to get. Then you know that this project will contribute NC 5,000 x 0.25 (NC 1,250) to the expenses every six months.

Take note that 0.25 is the decimal version for 25% which is another way of presenting $^{25}/_{100}$.

Then you may have other one off costs such as purchase of mobile phones for project officers and let us estimate that 2 mobile phones would cost NC 15,000 together.

The next stage is then to bring up the subtotals together. This will give us the following picture for a three year project:

Internet bill: NC 625 per month x 12 = NC 7,500 per year
Phone bill: NC 3,000 per month x 12 = NC 36,000 per year
Courier: NC 3,000 per month x 12 = NC 36,000 per year
Maintenance: NC 1,250 every six months x 2 = NC 2,500 per year
Cost of mobile phones: NC 15, 000

This will give you a total of **NC 97,000** for project communication in one year and we take this as year one of the project. The second and third years will not capture the one off cost one mobile phones (NC 15,000) purchased in year one, so ideally the annual communication expenses for years two and three would have been **NC 82,000.** However, it is safe to factor in **inflationary changes** and as such you may estimate that costs would go up by 10% each year. That would have you pegging project communication budget for year two at **NC 90, 200** calculated from **[NC82, 000 x $^{110}/_{100}$ or NC 82,000 x 1.1]** and for year three at **NC 99,220** calculated from **[NC90, 200 x $^{110}/_{100}$ or NC 90,200 x 1.1]**

This process goes on for each of the budget items. Some donors require this detail for each sub item while for others just indicating the total project communication cost is fine but still have your details on hand to show whoever queries that you did your homework.

Preference in terms of the level of detail of the budget differs from one donor to another. However, for your own convenience at planning and implementation level, make sure that your budget is self-explanatory and simplistic. Below are three modes of presentation of the budget which must all be prepared.

Budget Mode A - Detailed budget showing overall totals per budget item for the whole project duration

Table 6 Sample of detailed budget

BUDGET LINES		AMOUNT NC
Community Mobilization	Baseline studies (meals & accommodation, transport & stationery for three team members for 20 days)	
	Mobilizing community structures (meals & accommodation, transport & stationery for three staff for 20 days)	
	Project orientation and leadership training for community committees (20 participants & four facilitators workshop facilitators for five days)	
Community Support	Facilitator (meals & accommodation) @ NC2000/day for 12 days/mo for 18 mo	
	1 Facilitator's salary @ NC 300/mo for 18mo	
	Community awareness meetings	
	Bicycles for community volunteers	
Project Publicity	Promotion material (T/Shirts; brochures; posters)	
Transportation	Fuel and lubricants	
	Maintenance	
Monitoring and Evaluation	Monitoring visits	
	Board meetings	
	Evaluation	
Networking	Project related meetings with other players	
	Network membership	
Project Documentation	Stationery	
	Computer and accessories maintenance	
Project Communication	Phone, fax, postal, internet, maintenance	**286,420**
TOTAL		
Administration	15% of total	
GRAND TOTAL		

Budget Mode B - Summary budget showing main headings of budget items only broken down by year

Table 7 Sample of summary budget with main headings

Budget Line Item	Year 1	Year 2	Year 3	Overall
Community Mobilisationn				
Community Support				
Project Publicity				
Transportation				
Monitoring and Evaluation				
Networking				
Project Communication	**NC 97,000**	**NC 90,200**	**NC 99,220**	NC 286,420
TOTAL				
Administration				
Grand Total				

Budget Mode C – Detailed budget showing headings and sub headings of budget items broken down by year

Table 8 Sample of summary budget with main headings and sub headings

Budget Line Item	Year 1	Year 2	Year 3	Overall
Community Mobilisation				
Baseline studies				
Mobilising community structures				
Project orientation and leadership training for community committees				
Community Support				
Meals & Subsistence				
Project Officer's Salary				
Community Awareness Meetings				
Bicycles for Community Volunteers				
Project Publicity				
Promotion material (T/Shirts; brochures; posters)				
Transportation				
Fuel and lubricants				
Maintenance				

Monitoring and Evaluation				
Monitoring visits				
Board meetings				
Evaluation				
Networking				
Project related meetings				
Network membership				
Project Documentation				
Stationery				
Computer and accessories maintenance				
Project Communication	**NC 97,000**	**NC 90,200**	**NC 99,220**	**NC 286,420**
Internet bill	NC 7,500	NC 8,250	NC 9,075	NC 24,825
Phone bill	NC 36,000	NC 39,600	NC 43,560	NC 119,160
Courier	NC 36,000	NC 39,600	NC 43,560	NC 119,160
Maintenance	NC 2,500	NC 2,750	NC 3,025	NC 8,275
Mobile phone purchase	NC 15,000	-	-	NC 15,000
TOTAL				
Administration				
Grand Total				

Quite often certain activities are overlooked because they are deemed more institutional than project based yet the project needs them. Let us look at the costs on meetings of the board; I have heard NGOs claiming that their board members could not meet because they had no funds. But if you have projects running it is better to present your case in a project proposal that board meetings have a direct bearing on the way project resources are being managed. A case can be made that a scheduled meeting of the board is a monitoring activity and projects should be able to support such activities under the monitoring and evaluation (M & E) budget line. But then this has to be factored in the proposal and clearly mentioned in that narrative of the technical proposal so that the funders are aware of your case and intensions. For instance if you have four projects running and the normal practice is that there would be four board meetings, the costs could be spread over the four project budgets for each to support at least one board meeting in a year under the M & E budget. The bottom line is that this must be planned for when developing the project proposals. Some funders have been known to be very understanding.

Another aspect that may suffer if not well presented and negotiated is that of networking. NGOs belong to various networks some of which require subscription fees. For an NGO that is already pressed financially due to restrictions on project funds provided by donors, it may be difficult to benefit from such networks. It is therefore useful for NGOs to present their case clearly and justify the importance of network expenses primarily in relation to the projects they are proposing to a donor. It is more likely to ease your case through if you explain to the donor in what ways a budget line on networking would be beneficial to the project. Oftentimes certain budget lines are declined by donors because they have not been justified and give the impression that they were put in just to increase the budget.

Maintaining healthy relationships with donors

Resource mobilization is not an event; it does not end with acquisition of funding. This is a process; therefore it is important that NGOs continue to attach importance to the whole value chain. They must make the effort of creating fertile ground for breeding a sustainable relationship with the funders right from the point of first contact. The next sections share some tips on how NGOs can achieve that under various situations.

Some Notes on Meetings with donors and follow ups

Meetings with donors are inevitable in the course of resource mobilization and it is important that the organization prepares well for such meetings. The following are some of the key tips that representatives need to be aware of:

- When meeting funders it is normal that some sense of fear may emerge (they have the power of the money) but the fear has to be managed

- It is important to keep to time when meeting donors

- If you are given a chance to present your proposal at the meeting with them, be aware that you would normally have very limited time and hence you must prepare your presentation well.

- Power Point is in common use nowadays

- Donors are particularly interested in key areas and this may include the objectives, background and budget

- The first few minutes/the first three pages are most important for you to sell the organization to donors – instant impression can keep momentum of their attention. Mention you funders on the first page

- Show them you know your subject

- Don't give a breakdown of the budget, just mention the total figure

- When challenged on issues, remember that defense of the proposal is key and it is your responsibility, don't be too quiet, be assertive but don't defend the indefensible. Good judgment is key

54

- If there is more than one representative from your organization make sure you speak the same language in terms of the contents of the proposal…be complementary rather than contradictory

- Never assume the donors know. Give or make available the information

- Make sure you answer all questions asked by the donor. This shows that you are prepared

- Diplomacy is important to ensure you do not annoy your donors

- During closing remarks show them that you followed and understood their feedback

Progress updates

There are two types of updates that can be made to donors. The first type is mandatory and this is in form of activity and financial progress reports at the prescribed frequency agreed upon by the donor and your organization. Make sure that your project team coordinates well and prepares reports that are clear in their content as far as project progress is concerned. The reports must also be submitted in good time. Anytime there is a delay, the donor must be informed in advance but this should not be a habit. There must be credible justification for any delays. Good presentation of reports and on time reflects your level of organization and builds a good track record in the eyes of the donor. The benefits of this go beyond your relationship with that donor. They may actually recommend you to other donors. Do not forget that donors share notes.

While the first type of updates is common knowledge to NGO, the second type is most often overlooked or considered unimportant. Take for instance, a newspaper article or a radio programme which talks about your organization's work and its impact on the lives of people you serve; is that not an update worth sharing with your donors? Letting them know that the work your organization does is being recognized, gives them greater confidence in your organization and assurance that they have invested their funds with a right partner. There could also be other updates such as recruitment of a new board member or a visit by a high profile personality to your organization. You may even include a statement they made about your organization.

Updating donors does not have to be biased towards glossy news only. There are important unfortunate events that occur in the life of an organization and these should also be reported. There may be instance of fraud, a break in or an industrial related issue which may place your organization's public image in a light of discomfort but it is a mark of honesty if your donors are updated by yourselves instead of hearing it from the grapevine or from the media.

Crediting your donor

Always ensure that your donor is credited on all stories or publications related to the project. For instance if media people ask for an interview in relation to a project that a certain donor is funding, you must make sure that such a donor is acknowledged in the interviews being given. If you have some publications coming up under a particular project with a donor, credits must be given. Some donors specifically place this as a demand in the funding agreement while others may not be explicit but that does not mean they do not need credits.

Types of donors

The main funding institutions can be grouped in three categories namely bilateral donors, multilateral donors and foundations.

Bilateral aid is defined as support from one government directly to the government of another country e.g. from Japan to Kenya while multilateral aid is that which comes from several countries but is channeled through international agencies such as the United Nations. On the other hand, foundations are private charitable institutions whose main focus is philanthropy, in other places they are referred to as trusts. Some of these grant making institutions are established by wealthy individuals or corporations. At the end of this book there is a list of foundations that focus on international philanthropy. Within your own national jurisdictions you can also find local foundations.

The sections below examine the advantages and disadvantages associated with each category of donors. This is useful to know and consider when you are planning your fundraising programmes.

Advantages of bilateral aid

It can be more focused and readily available with minimized competition because the donor governments will have specified which countries they are going to work with regardless of the interests they have in choosing those countries.

Challenges with bilateral aid

Such aid is subject to unexpected changes on conditions and duration because of changing political or economic landscapes in the funding countries. It is easy for the donor to impose its agenda on the recipient organization. Such agenda may border on political, economic or diplomatic interests of the donor country.

It can also be bureaucratic in terms of accessing funding.

Advantages of multilateral aid

Multilateral funding is more likely to be devoid of restrictive conditions that cause undue pressure bordering on political, economic or diplomatic interests of a particular country. This is because resources have been pooled from various countries that among themselves have a diversity of interests, which are sometimes conflicting.

Challenges with multilateral donors

The geographical scope is broader and competition may be high
It can also be bureaucratic in terms of accessing funding.

Advantages of foundations

There procedures for processing funding are usually less arduous
They generally operate on more flexible terms

Challenges with of foundations

Usually funding may be of smaller budgets than the other two.

In conclusion, this chapter has revealed and cemented the argument raised at the beginning that resource mobilization is serious business and does not happen by accident. There is effort that has to be applied, time must be spent, skills applied and resource allocated to plan and implement resource mobilization effectively. The chapter has also showcased the various types of funding sources and has shared practical ideas on how plan and implement resource mobilization. Dealing with donors is not a one day job and does not end with signing a funding agreement. The relationship has to be nurtured and should be looked at as an investment.

Indeed the indigenous NGO must happen to resource mobilization and not the other way.

Chapter Three

Case Studies and Lessons From Other NGOs in the Developing World

This chapter presents some case studies on resource mobilization approaches that have applied the business model among NGOs in the developing world. These case studies are not from another planet. They are real and have made a difference in those NGOs in different corners of the developing world be it Africa, Asia or Latin America. The chapter also summarizes some important lessons for the broader NGO family in the developing world.

BRAC from Bangladesh

Established in 1972 and at the time known as the Bangladesh Rehabilitation Assistance Committee (BRAC), BRAC presents one of the most inspiring stories to have emerged from the developing world as far as NGO resource mobilization is concerned. BRAC is a massive NGO established by Sir Fazle Hasan Abed and operating across nine countries across Asia and Africa. As at May 2010, the NGO was employing 120,000 people and serving 110 million people. At the centre of its philosophy is empowering citizens to move from mere aid recipients to control their own destiny.

BRAC is 73% self-financed having invested in commercial enterprises such as dairy and food projects, a retail chain of stores selling handcrafts. Fowler (1997) reports that back in 1994, BRAC generated 31% of its revenue from business enterprises; compare that with the situation in 2011 where such revenue has grown by 42 percentage points! The NGO now has offices in 14 countries including the United States of America (USA) and the United Kingdom (UK). BRAC's revenue between 2009 and 2011 was as follows:

Year	2009	2010	2011
Amount (US$)	460,000,000	495,000,000	572,000,000

Starting as a relief and rehabilitation project in 1972 after the Bangladesh Liberation War of 1971, BRAC was set up to help returning refugees and eventually evolved into service provider in microcredit. It also focused on community development programmes such as agriculture, fisheries, cooperatives, health and family planning. With foresighted leadership, BRAC established a research and evaluation division (RED) in 1975 to provide a mechanism for feedback, knowledge management and planning of its programmes. By 1977 the NGO was able to reorganize its approach and the institutional set up at community level through which it rendered its services. This was followed by the establishment of a commercial printing press to finance its activities.

> BRAC has done what few others have – they have achieved success on a massive scale, bringing life-saving health programmes to millions of the world's poorest people. They remind us that even the most intractable health problems are solvable, and inspire us to match their success throughout the developing world

Bill Gates – Co-chair

Sir Fazle Hasan Abed, founder and chairman of BRAC was Knighted by Queen Elizabeth II in 2010 for his outstanding contribution to the alleviation of poverty. He used his income from the sale of his flat in London to set up BRAC. He lived in London after circumstances forced him to leave Bangladesh when the Liberation War had started in 1971. He was trained in Dhaka, Bangladesh, Glasgow and in London in the UK.

> We prize efficiency. We are run more like a business, with targets to be achieved, although there is no bottom line in the sense of a profit motive. But in everything we do, there are targets, whether it is to reduce child mortality rates or increase the numbers of children attending school.

Below is a list of enterprises in which BRAC has invested and managed to generated revenue to fund its core programmes while offering employment to many vulnerable people in society:

1. Retail

The *Aarong* Retail Chain of Stores is a unique and recognizable brand selling clothing, linen, shoes and home décor products among others. Established in 1978, *Aarong* earned US$ 30 Million in 2008 with a profit margin of US$ 5 million while in 2011 the total income was US$ 51.5 Million with a profit margin of US$ 8.5 Million. Aarong employs over 65,000 artisans with women comprising 85% of the staff.

2. Livestock and Fisheries

The NGO runs *BRAC Dairy* to provide fair price for milk to members of BRAC's Village Organisations (VOs) who invested micro loans received from BRAC for cows. BRAC Dairy was established to facilitate market linkages and protect price volatility from over-supply. Overall a milk volume amounting to 314.73 million litres was collected from its collection and chilling points.

A programme on *Artificial Insemination* is a support mechanism to the *BRAC Dairy* with over 2000 artificial inseminators employed and operating under the supervision of Veterinary experts. The artificial insemination programme is aimed at improving the livestock breed with the ultimate goal increasing milk production and by extension cattle population in Bangladesh.

BRAC Poultry has contributed significantly to the development of the poultry industry in Bangladesh. Producing day old chicks, running a diagnostic laboratory and providing support to poultry farmers, this venture has created income generating activities to millions of the rural poor in the country and in 2008 it distributed 9.3 million day old chicks

BRAC Feed Mills produces quality feed for poultry, fish and cattle and hence supports the poultry, dairy and aquaculture industries.

BRAC Broiler Processing Plant was established to meet the increasing demand for dressed chickens in major urban centres. This is the largest and sole automated plant in Bangladesh and buys chickens from BRAC's Poultry Rearing Farms and other selected sources
BRAC Fisheries supplies commercial fish farms with fish spawn, and fingerlings. With dwindling stock of fish in the wild, commercial farms have increasingly emerged and ***BRAC Fisheries*** is such an important player with its hatcheries.

3. Health

BRAC Salt industries produces iodised salt while the Sanitary Napkin & Delivery Kit centre aims at increasing women's hygienic behavior with the help of BRAC health volunteers.

4. Agriculture

BRAC Cold Storage facility was established with the support of UNDP and provides storage of potatoes for farmers who grow them in a region that produces very good harvest but lack proper post-harvest storage. The stored potatoes also act as surety to their owners who could access loans of up to 60% of the value of their stored potatoes as of 2012.

BRAC Tea Estates are part of the income generating portfolio for the organization with the surplus being directed to development programmes. With a staff profile of 3,000, the estates produced 16,000, 366 kilogrammes of tea in 2008.

Sericulture venture organizes women to undertake mulberry cultivation, silkworm and seed production, reeling and spinning of silk yarn and weaving and marketing silk. Up to 7500 women have been involved raising of silkworms with another 5,800 involved in spinning.

BRAC Horticulture aims to produce seedlings of high quality and making them available throughout the country. With 15 large horticulture nurseries spread across Bangladesh, BRAC distributes seedlings of good quality all over.

5. BRAC Printers and Packaging

Printers This desk top publishing facility produces 80% of its materials for BRAC's educational programme and official requirements while it also produces calendars, diaries and university publications among others. The **Packaging** service is done by BRAC Printing Pack manufactures packaging materials.

6. Alternative Energy and Renewables
This involves production of biogas, recycled handmade paper and solar power

Lessons for other NGOs

The case study here reveals what innovation can do. There are no limits to our imagination if we let sustained belief prevail in what we set out to do. Simply put, NGOs in the developing world should think outside the box and take away their inferiority complex. BRAC, an NGO from a developing country of Bangladesh is the world's (**mark the word "world's"**) largest NGO. From the case studies we can appreciate the fact that the NGOs have harnessed exceptional entrepreneurial innovation within the areas of their core business. Looking at IBASE we see that they have used IT to facilitate access to other like-minded organizations thereby enhancing the capacity of such organizations to promote their agenda while at the same time IBASE is able to generate revenue. The organisation's research credentials in policy and advocacy for its own work have enabled it to attract clients requiring services in similar thematic areas in various corners of the country as well as at the WSF. The case of BRAC shows that some of its enterprises have a social focus with its target constituencies being the central beneficiaries. For instance, BRAC Dairy has members of its VOs as major players and beneficiaries in milk production. Other enterprises also reveal more innovation through the creation of product value chain. For example BRAC Dairy has links with BRAC Artificial Insemination as a way of cattle population increase just like BRAC Feed Mills produces feed for cattle, fish and poultry. All these linkages are a manifestation of well thought through and researched business development processes.

Ability to learn and unlearn is a key characteristic of genuine leadership committed to change processes. BRAC despite all its economic success and its life span of close to forty years has remained relevant to its constituency. This has come about because the leadership has generated legacies of sensing and acknowledging the changes in the context in which they are operating. BRAC successfully moved from a relief and rehabilitation organization to development organization and even set up a research and evaluation department (RED) to facilitate feedback processes. Setting up RED itself was not enough as it could have been easily used for window dressing but the willingness to receive and accept feedback and respond to that feedback through change is an exceptional attitude worth emulating.

Credibility is another cornerstone for an NGO that wants to engage in social enterprise. This credibility should firstly be visible in the application of an organization's core business. UNDP supported the establishment of a cold storage at BRAC and the establishment of an internet node in collaboration with the Italian government at IBASE (a Brazilian NGO) because of the credibility that the two organizations had displayed in their work. NGOs in the developing world must be accountable on the resources they receive from donors and must also display professional seriousness coupled with the passion to make a real and not cosmetic difference. Moreover, organizations that are able to show genuine results in their core businesses and apply professionalism in their work, recruitment processes and utilization of resources will endure less labor in trying to attract support from existing and new donors and that support could not only come for direct social services but also social enterprises.

There are a lot of business opportunities for NGOs to embark on; the barrier is creativity. The existing mental models at institutional level, especially in management have a major influence on how the organization designs its financial plans. Leadership foresight is important in moving NGOs towards financial autonomy. The case studies also reveal to us that engaging in the domain of what is generally believed to be that of the private sector is possible and there is nothing wrong with it as long as the NGOs engage in fair practices and plough back surplus revenue into the organizations to promote their not-for-profit missions.

Other case studies – a general overview

While BRAC has been a phenomenal case study on a grand scale, it should be appreciated that other NGOs in different parts of the developing world have made good attempts as well to raise their own income besides relying on donors. Such NGOs and those that have not made any attempts yet will indeed pluck a leaf of golden lessons from BRAC. During the research on this book, the author came across several initiatives by NGOs across the developing world. The main challenge was the level of sophistication but nothing could be taken away from their creativity.

A youth NGO in Southern Africa has used some of its assets to generate revenue in various ways within the framework of the projects supported by donors. For instance this NGO has its own offices and it has been able to negotiate with some donors to have the projects they support pay for office space to be used by the projects. In the same way, some projects supported by donors and implemented through this youth organization, have hired assets from it to be used by the projects. Such assets include the public address system which is regularly used in awareness projects; institutional vehicles i.e. not tied to any funded project and these are rented out to projects which have not provided vehicles. In this respect the organization has operated as a separate system from the projects and offers its services to the projects at competitive rates. The projects pay the organization for use of the facilities and the revenue is transferred from project accounts into organization's accounts. It should be stated though that not all donors have entertained this, as in some cases, the facilities have been presented as the organization's contribution to the projects. Nevertheless, the value of that revenue has been phenomenal.

Further to this, the organization has a youth centre programme which was established with funding from the Australian Government, and partnership with the local City Council and the surrounding community. The youth centre is at the core of the organization's mission of promoting productive lives for youth using life skills approach. Apart from the sporting facilities, the centre has a conference room, a computer resource centre and other recreational facilities such as a restaurant. The youth organization has managed to utilize the facilities for social services to the youth while at the same time building business enterprises around them for its own income generation. Projects implemented by organization hire the conference room when they need to conduct training and stakeholder meetings locally. The conference package includes use of the restaurant for meals. The sporting facilities have also attracted major sports clubs within the city and those visiting the city for sporting activities. Such clubs continue hiring the facilities for their preparations at a fee. In 2009 the organization entered into partnership with UNICEF where the latter provided scholarships to disadvantaged girls to learn computer skills at the resource centre for free. UNICEF in turn paid the youth organization for the girls' tuition and use of facilities during the lessons.

In conclusion to this chapter, we see that there are unlimited possibilities with imagination. Even donors can reward innovation if it has real social benefits to the constituents of the NGO.

Chapter Four

Access and Usage Of Unrestricted Funds: Some Ideas

In preceding chapters, some case studies have been shared to showcase innovation and resolve in resource mobilization by some indigenous NGOs in the developing world. This chapter expands on the lessons from such innovation and resolve by sharing more ideas with a bias on sources of funding which is unrestricted. This has been done on purpose to consolidate the place of nontraditional sources of funding in the minds of decision makers in NGOs.

There are so many innovative ideas being implemented by various NGOs. As established from the case studies and the ensuing lessons learnt, thinking out of the box and professionalizing the organization are very central features for an organization that wants to move forward in terms of commercial enterprises. It is important that the organization is clear as to what enterprises it can or cannot engage is based on their values and beliefs. This then can lead to a well-documented investment policy for the organization for everyone to know how far they can go when planning investments for the organization. This is explained in the subsequent sections.

Some suggestions for revenue generation from social enterprises activities

Below is a brainstormed list of commercial ventures in which NGOs can engage to raise unrestricted revenue. Some are more familiar and self-explanatory while others may be less familiar and therefore require further explanation. You will therefore notice that some have received bias in terms of explanation. This is based on the author's discretion. The list is not exhaustive.

Shareholding: The stock market refers to the business of buying and selling stock. When one owns all or part of the stock in a particular company, it means they own part of the company. Each part of the company in that respect is called a share and as such any owner of part or of the stock is called a shareholder. NGOs can invest money in a company that is listed and become shareholders. If the company registers profit, the stakeholders may share the profit in form of dividends.

Property development: Investments into property may include buying or constructing houses and office space which can then be let out to generate income for the organization.

Hospitality: The hospitality industry is one area in which NGOs are regular customers and they could capitalize on that need. If an NGO owns conferencing or accommodation facilities such as guest houses or fully fledged lodges, they can avail them to the wider public apart from making a solidarity appeal among the NGOs themselves to patronize the facilities.

Transportation and car hire: There are various models for transport services that NGOs can invest in. For example, some NGOs own trucks or even smaller vehicles that are then hired out. Car hiring is an essential service and has higher potential in areas where the tourism industry is growing or is big.

Consultancy: as an NGO operating in a particular sector, your team may have acquired specialized skills and knowledge in that sector and these could be availed to other NGOs on a consultancy basis. IBASE of Brazil is able to provide consultancy services in socioeconomic research on a range of aspects such as baseline studies, policy analysis etc.

Publications: Some organizations produce publications as part of their programme service extension and/or public relations. Some are funded by donors while others are self funded. Such publications may be sold to the general public and raise some revenue; besides that, some advertising can also be integrated to raise further income. If your publication is funded by a donor, you need to negotiate clearance first.

Internet advertising: More and more NGOs are now running their own websites and this has enhanced their visibility. This medium can be used to entice advertisers onto the website and enable your organization access some revenue. If your website is funded by a donor, you need to check whether they would be comfortable with the arrangement or not.

Gift shop: General merchandise can be stocked targeting tourists and item collectors or providing basic goods targeting low income groups at fair prices. Some NGOs have used gift shops to sell items which represent their core values e.g. an environmental NGO stocking non-timber forest products (NTFP) such as honey, wild fruit juices etc. Others may sell timber forest products harvested from sustainable sources.

Pay toilet/public convenience: can be more suitable for NGOs involved in sanitation and hygiene though any NGOs with appropriate business acumen can do it.

Recreational services: an NGO may develop sporting facilities or children's entertainment facilities and charge for their use.

Screen printing: printing of banners, T/Shirts, stickers etc.

Public appeals: Can be done through various media such as newspapers, internet, television or radio. Some media houses provide free space/slots for nonprofit causes. Arrangements with supermarkets or restaurants can also help to collect money from the general public through donation tins or boxes placed by the tills and clearly labeled.

Competitions: various competitions can be organized to raise money e.g. SMS promotions are becoming common in some parts of the developing world. The SMS promotions have a dual purpose of enhancing your public relations besides the financial benefits that may come.

Sports tournaments: this is one of the avenues where NGOs can engage more closely with the corporate world. There is a common culture in the corporate world to sponsor golf teams and tournaments in general. Social football is also popular in other parts of the developing world. NGOs can organize such tournaments to tap into that money while promoting their cause.

Cause related marketing: An NGO can work with a specific company that sells an item and also lets the consumer know that a percentage of the price is given to the NGO
.

Others: Desktop publishing; Public address system; Maize mill; Bakery; IT Support services: business centre (photocopying, internet café); farming/Filling station/service garage and driving school

Reserve funds and Endowment funds

The concepts of reserve funds and endowment funds are another novel way for raising unrestricted funds in NGOs. They have been given special consideration in this chapter with some case studies because they remain untapped sources with the indigenous NGO family in the developing world. These concepts are totally strange to most of the NGO leaders and they have been explained here to demystify them so that they can be exploited and embraced fully for the benefit of the NGOs and their constituents.

Reserve funds

Reserve funds are those that accumulate from surplus generated through revenue generating activities such as those outlined above. Such funds are kept for use in emergency situations, "rainy days" so to speak. Investopedia defines a reserve fund as an account set aside by an individual or business to meet any unexpected costs that may arise in the future as well as the future costs of upkeep. In most cases the fund is a savings account or another highly liquid asset, as it is impossible to predict when an unexpected cost may arise.

It is not uncommon that in the life of an NGO unexpected costs may arise due to various factors. Sometimes disbursement of funds from a donor may delay for various reasons while certain project activities are time or season specific e.g. procurement and supply of farm inputs under rain fed conditions. NGOs with reserve funds available may lend money to such project activities and get refunded when the disbursement has finally been done. One of the NGOs I researched on was the Active Youth Initiative for Social Enhancement (AYISE) who had a six month drought of funding between September 2008 and April 2009. By September 2008, almost all the projects they had been implementing were winding up and the next funding contracts had been discussed but none was immediately available until April 2009. Here is a scenario where the NGO had done all its homework in securing further funding but it did not have control over the timing of the funding, the donors had. Six months of drought is not a small time challenge more specially for an NGO in the developing world, but the amazing story of AYISE is worth emulating because this organization did not collapse. They were able to maintain some key staff through the reserve funds they had generated from various enterprises. They had an umbrella when the rainy day had arrived!

Endowment funds

Investopedia defines an endowment fund as an investment fund set up by an institution in which regular withdrawals from the invested capital are used for ongoing operations or other specified purposes. It further explains that endowment funds are often used by non profits, universities, hospitals and churches. Endowments are designed to keep the principal amount intact while using the investment income from dividends for charitable efforts. The Resource Alliance clarifies this concept further here stating that an endowment fund is used to generate investment income for charitable purposes while the underlying capital asset is not available to be spent but only the interest earned.

It provides stability because it provides regular income over the long term and reduces an organization's dependency.

It also enhances a nonprofit's credibility in the eyes of donors because it gives them confidence that the organization is going to be there for a long time.

How can such capital be sourced?

Most nonprofits that have set up endowment funds access the capital from donors and supporters but since an endowment can be started with any amount of money, however small, you may raise funds from income generating activities. However, in any case, building an endowment is a long term project.

If you are raising money for your endowment from donors, you need to prepare your case properly so that there is a solid explanation to the potential donors on why you are setting it up and how you plan to use the endowment and its earnings. It is also important to learn from those organizations accessible to you that may already be operating endowment funds. Also bear in mind that fundraising for endowment is separate from fundraising for immediate needs. Ensure that your organization has taken or is taking care of fundraising for immediate needs before engaging in endowment fundraising. In this case your income other commercial enterprises may provide revenue to support emergencies in the short term. These are called *reserve funds*. On the other hand you should be working on the endowment to eventually address needs in the long term.

Not every donor is a prospect for supporting endowments and as such you need to do your homework properly. Some individuals who support endowments do so because they are interested in leaving a legacy and providing for the long term future of the organizations they support; and in such cases wills and bequests become the main component for endowment fundraising.

Let us have a practical feel of how an endowment fund works with these case studies below. The case studies take us through some of the successes and challenges an endowment fund may experience.

Mulanje Mountain Conservation Trust (MMCT) – Malawi

MMCT was established in the mid 1990s as an environmental endowment trust and works with Malawi Government's Department of Forestry in the ensuring participatory and sustainable conservation of biodiversity and natural resources in the Mulanje Mountain Forest Reserve in Southern Malawi, in Southern Africa. MMCT was originally funded by the Global Environmental Facility through the World Bank, which provided capital for its endowment fund.

Here is an excerpt from the 2009/2010 Annual Report of the Mulanje Mountain Conservation Trust (MMCT) as presented by its Executive Director, Mr Carl Bruessow

The MMCT endowment has endured volatile value movements in concert with the economic shocks being experienced on the global markets. The historic high of the MMCT endowment account...of US$6.2 million declined due to withdrawals and market losses to US$4.9 million in the depths of the US banking crisis. It recovered strongly in 2009 with a 24.96% return and due to the agreement with Norway allowing the trust to fully reinvest, steadily recovered again to US$6 million in early 2010. This most encouraging rebound from the financial crisis was then impacted by the European states economic instability, with the value taking a further sharp downturn in April 2010 to UsS$5.7 million. The account again fully recovered and as of the 15th July visit of the UBS asset manager now shows a balance of over US$ 6 million. This is a new account high, adjusted for withdrawals, and represents asset management in the top 10% of the endowment category, with returns for the past three years better than that of Yale, Harvard or the Gates Foundation, much larger organizations with better economies of scale.

Once a year, the Governors interact on a personal level with the UBS Financial Services fund manager visiting from Seattle, Washington to appreciate the state and future prospects of the MMCT endowment.

Child Rights and You (CRY) – India[3]

The Child Rights and You (CRY) originally Child Relief and YOU, is an Indian NGO established in 1979 with the purpose of restoring basic rights to food, shelter, health and education to deprived children of India. The late Rippan Kapur teamed up with a group of friends and family to establish CRY. The NGO catalyzes change in the lives of underprivileged children. Its mission is to enable society take responsibility for the situation of the deprived Indian child and so motivate them to seek resolution through individual and collective action. In that way children are enabled to realize their full potential. Partially modeled along UNICEF approach, CRY has developed with enlisting public support through sales of greeting cards and donations. It has also gone into sales of calendars, address books and stationery. CRY Child Development Corpus Fund in 1987 to ensure the stability of the organization and, more importantly, of its support to project partners and inflows. Individuals, companies, trusts and associations can donate to this fund which may not be used directly to support CRY projects but must be invested in government approved securities. The interest earned from the endowment fund investments is used for CRY's support activities.

Endowment fund donations accounted for 16.9% of total resources mobilized in 1992-93, and in the financial year 1993-94, the corpus fund was expected to grow to approximately 17.5 million Rupees (US$557,813).

Foundation for Higher Education (Foundacion para la Educacion Superior – FES) – Colombia[4]

Foundacion para la Educacion Superior was founded in 1964 to help a public university meets its cash flow and programme expenses. Following habitually delayed government disbursements, the University frequently found itself borrowing from local banks at high interest rates. At the same time funding from foreign sources was

---

[3] Source: Synergos Institute
[4] Source: Synergos Institute

being deposited in local banks without earning interest and following advice from such foreign sources contributing to the University, FES was set up as a mechanism that would also promote donations from alumni and local business community. Besides contributions from FES's founding members, the Ford Foundation provided a seed grant while the Rockefeller and Kellogg Foundations committed to channel their grants to the University through FES to allow it make use of the earned interest. FES became independent of the University in the early 1970S and its reach broadened and FES's Vice Presidency for Social Development (VPSD) was established to make grants, conduct research and create seed programmes outside the original university.

FES grew with the understanding that it had to generate its own endowment and enough funds to pursue its mission. In the first stage of its development, FES acquired the financial expertise to manage the funds that the university received from US foundation sources. It loaned these funds to local businesses, sharing the return on a basis of 75% for the programme and 25% for FES. In this way the foundation increased its own endowment while supporting programmes at the university. At the same time FES received savings from local sources that trusted the foundation as their money management agent and earned a differential interest.

Two internal factors determined the development of FES' financial expertise; the active participation of bankers and business people from the community on the Board and the professionalization of its staff in financial management. When it became a CFC (Compania de Financiamiento Comercial) or commercial financing company in 1975, it increased its ability to received deposits from outside sources. At some point there was tension created between those managing or committed to the financial side of FES and those managing or committed to the social development mission of FES. This dilemma had emerged because the Board had intended to grow the endowment from its small initial capital and others perceived this as placing limited priority to philanthropic endevours. Changing national regulations have at times affected FES's endowment fund; once in the mid-1990s, Colombian Law was enacted limiting the use of permanent funds as part of technical capital to 50%. This limitation (removed shortly afterwards) would have confined FES's capacity to receive deposits and make a profit on the differential interest for its loans.

Table 9 Growth of FES's Endowment and Funds (in US$ average exchange)

Year	Total Value (including PMF)	Permanent (Restricted) Funds
1965	2,667	-
1970	218,872	65,050
1980	5,615,060	2,183,693
1990	22,892,890	10,617,443
1994	42,663,025	14,676,296

FES evolved into a corporate structure first by consolidating of the Foundation into a CFC. The corporate structure is controlled and owned by Fundacion-FES. FES and its affiliates offer multi-banking services as permitted by Colombia's financial sector regulations. Some of the affiliates are: CORFES, SA an investment bank; FIDURES SA, fiduciary entity managing third party money; FES Leasing SA, a leasing corporation and FES Valores SA, a stock brokerage house.

Lessons from the case studies

Financial expertise is necessary to manage the funds. This can be done through outsourcing the fund management function as MMCT is doing with UBS or may be developed internally as has happened with FES and CRY.

Global events are intertwined with successes or challenges of your endowment. The global financial crisis that began in the USA and the economic instability affecting the Eurozone have their impacts.

Management should enhance its financial literacy to be able to understand and interpret the situation related to organizational funds and investments.

Donors become more confident in supporting your organization because operating an endowment fund reflects a high level of competences. By doing that, your organization has a better chance of reinvesting its interests during the periods that donor funding is able to cover expenses that would otherwise have been covered by the endowment fund income.

Understanding the regulations of the country where your NGO is based is also very crucial because that will inform you where to and not to invest your funds without running into trouble with the Law

Policies governing reserve funds, endowment funds and unrestricted funds in general

Setting up policies around commercial ventures, reserve funds and endowment funds is very important and the following guide from investopedia with additional input from the author is useful:

Investment policy: this policy guides the types of investments the NGO can make for its income generating activities and what an endowment fund manager can make and how aggressive he or she can be in meeting return targets.

Withdrawal policy: this policy determines the amount that the institution can take from the amount remaining in the fund. For an endowment fund, it is a "must" that a principle amount remains all the time. The word *must* is in inverted commas because in some countries there are no specific legislations governing endowment funds and such legal loopholes can lead to abuse. It therefore calls for moral high ground to adopt as a standard and moral practice what has been established as a legal benchmark in jurisdictions where endowment funds are well established.

Fund usage policy: this policy ensures that the money from the reserve fund and/or endowment fund is being used properly and for the purposes set out in the fund. Again, where there is no specific legal framework or where enforcement is weak, it is the responsibility of the organization to ensure high standards are maintained. Having a policy also helps control indiscriminate usage; for instance drawing a whole reserve account to pay staff bonuses at year end. Misjudgment on spending can come about because of excitement about the surplus and its "unrestricted" nature or because of ignorance of the moral obligations that come along with such revenue. Some of the ways in which such funds can be used are as follows:

- Meeting overhead expenses that donors have declined to support
- Acquiring other assets that become necessary to have with time but are not covered under any existing project
- Direct support to programme work

In general we should notice that the difference between a reserve fund and an endowment fund is that with the former, the money is held in reserve for emergencies and all of it may be spent and therefore may not provide stable long term earnings. On the other hand an endowment fund has a principle amount which is protected from withdrawal beyond the interest. Some even choose to withdraw only a portion of the interest in order the reinvest the rest of the interest.

In summary, we now can appreciate that there are many sources of unrestricted funds that NGOs can tap into. Some are simple to start while others are more complex and less known yet effective well cultivated. The chapter has further expanded on how unrestricted funds may be used. It is easy to get excited when your NGO has raised some revenue which is not under the strict eye of a donor and utilize it for less strategic expenditure. However, the nature of work for NGOs calls for a higher moral ground and high level of accountability to the public for whom the NGOs claims to exist.

Chapter Five

Understanding the Legal Framework on Resource Mobilization

Chapter two introduced the need for environmental scanning when planning for resource mobilization. Six parameters were introduced under PESTEL analysis. The environmental scanning revealed that the external environment is broad; however this chapter will focus on the aspect that is generally overlooked. Research on this book revealed that most NGO leaders were not conversant with the legal provisions governing the work of NGOs in their countries and more particularly those provisions to do with fundraising. An examination of the legal environment will go a long way in ensuring that organizations make their plans within the legislative framework of their countries. In a way this chapter is about raising awareness to NGO leaders on the importance of understanding the laws that govern their work.

> BRAC has been given political space when in other countries NGOs are not allowed to grow so big - Sir Fazle Hasan Abed, Founder and Chairman of BRAC, Bangladesh

While the financial future of NGOs in the developing world rests largely with the NGOs themselves in terms of capacity and attitude, the context in which they operate should also be examined when they are developing their resource mobilization plans.

The following passages discuss the prevailing legislative provisions sampled from various regions of the developing world and examine the impact that these provisions have on the work of NGOs in general and particularly resource mobilization. This discussion is largely based on the legal analysis conducted by the International Centre for Non Profit Law (ICNL) but has been adapted by the author, while some of it is based on the author's own analysis. While some legal environments have negative impacts, NGO leaders should not use this as a scapegoat because the overriding factor still remains

79

innovation and ability to learn and unlearn on the part of the leadership.

Case 1: Pakistan

The legal framework in Pakistan provides for freedom of NGOs to pursue public benefit purposes. Tax exemptions and fiscal benefits are available to certain NGOs depending on their purposes and activities. There are no legal barriers to operational activities and access to financial resources.

Case 2: Rwanda

In as far as resource mobilization is concerned; the law is conducive as it provides for NGOs to engage in any economic activity provided that funds generated through such economic activity are used for the non profit mission of the organization. NGOs are also exempt from tax on most categories. However in terms of operational, the law places some demands and restrictions on how NGOs go about their work. For instance Article 20 requires that the legal representatives of the NGO and their assistants must be approved by the Ministry of Justice and also that by law the NGOs must incorporate formal government priorities including the country's vision 2020 into their mission.

Case 3: Venezuela

There is generally an enabling environment for NGO work in Venezuela. There are no legal barriers to fundraising both externally and domestically. The key challenge is the exchange control regime where any donation must be converted to the local currency, Bolivars. This is enforced under the Illicit Currency Exchange Law. An NGO may carry out any lawful economic activity compatible with its aims and with its non-for-profit nature. The law being silent on this, the expert views state that Venezuelan courts require that NGOs pursue such activities as a means of advancing their non-profit goals, self sustainability, and financial autonomy. However the prevailing political climate affects the decisions by domestic donors in as far as funding human rights activities is concerned.

Case 4: Yemen

Yemen is said to have one of the best Laws in the Middle East/North Africa region governing NGOs. However government regularly threatens to amend the laws to make them restrictive because it does not approve of the role of NGOs in development, human rights and community participation. Moreover the Law on Money Laundering and Combating Terrorism passed in 2010 is deemed harmful to NGOs especially those with projects funded by external parties. The Law permits the Central Bank to conduct surveillance of bank funds, examining and inspecting bank accounts without prior notice.

Case 5: South Africa

The legal environment in South Africa is generally enabling and supportive of NGO activity. The Non Profit Organizations (NPO) Act of 1997 states that within the limits prescribed by law, every organ of state must determine and coordinate the implementation of its policies and measures in a manner designed to promote, support and enhance the capacity of NPOs to perform their functions. The law does not impose any constraints on the ability of NGOs to seek and secure funding (foreign or domestic). NGOs are permitted to carry out commercial activities either directly or through commercial subsidiaries. NGOs can also compete for government funding.

Case 6: Colombia

The CSOs in Colombia are strong and sophisticated, working in human rights peace building and women's rights among others. However the country has a web of laws, policies and regulations that are complicated and often contradictory and this makes it difficult to understand the legal framework for NGOs. In terms of access to financial resources, NGOs are permitted to acquire and dispose of property, invest resources, and import and export goods but the 1991

Constitution prohibits all branches of government to grant money or aid to private entities, including NGOs. This is aimed at discouraging corruption. However, NGOs may sign contracts with government entities to promote programmes and activities consistent with national and regional development plans as long as they have recognized qualifications.

Case 7: Ethiopia

Ethiopia's NGOs and civil society organizations (CSOs) in general have become important contributors to the country's political and economic renaissance. The 2009 Proclamation to Provide for the Registration and Regulation of Charities and Societies (CSP) is Ethiopia's first comprehensive law on NGOs and among other things, it restricts NGOs that receive more than 10% of their funding from foreign sources from engaging in essentially all human rights and advocacy activities. There is also excessive oversight on NGO activities by the law enforcement agency.

Case 8: Indonesia

Like most legal environments already explored above, Indonesian Law categorizes organizational forms in terms of registration. It identifies two categories namely associations and foundations. In its interpretation, associations are membership based while foundations are not. However this categorization transcends various aspects of regulation including resource mobilization in the sense that foundations are allowed to engage in commercial activities while associations are not permitted. Foundations can embark on commercial activities to support the attainment of their objectives by either enterprises or participating as shareholders in commercial enterprises. If a foundation sets up a commercial entity, the activities of the enterprise must relate to the foundation's statutory purpose. Shareholding by a foundation should not exceed 25% of the total value of its assets.

There are no legal impediments to raising foreign or domestic funds, however the law on foundations requires that if foundations receive more than 500 million Indonesian rupiah or more, they should be audited by a public accountant and should have their annual report summaries published in an Indonesian language daily newspaper.

The eight legal analyses provided above are based on information sourced from the ICNL while the analysis below is based on the author's assessment of the Malawi NGO Act.

Case 9: Malawi

The NGO Act of 2000 provides freedom for NGOs to raises funds from both domestic and foreign sources. The specific provision on fundraising is stated as follows:

> Every NGO registered under this Act, including an exempt organisation which is registered, may solicit and accept funds and contributions and engage in public fundraising for the furtherance of its public benefit purposes as it may deem appropriate, subject to compliance with the reporting requirements prescribed under this Act, or any other written law.

The Law also provides that an NGO can only be registered by the NGO board after it has been registered by the NGO coordinating body (CONGOMA) which is itself a self- regulating body and also approved by the Ministry responsible for the activities to be undertaken by the NGO in the form of a memorandum of understanding or any other agreement between the Ministry and the NGO. If an NGO's registration has been cancelled or suspended by the NGO Board, it has the right to seek judicial redress as the law is clear that *any NGO aggrieved by a decision of the Board made under this part may apply to the High Court for judicial review.*

The legal restriction of the law, though not enforced aggressively is that any registered NGO must supply its audited annual financial statements, its annual report outlining the activities undertaken by the NGO in the year and such other information as may be prescribed, its source of funding among others.

Commentary on the legal frameworks governing NGOs

The legal analyses present some interesting insights which may challenge perceptions that some readers may have had based on what they hear from or read in the media. Different countries have designed their legislation motivated by various reasons ranging from political to social. Talking about political environments, it is noted that these are either reflected directly in the laws or indirectly in practice. In Ethiopia the political thinking is reflected in the law while in Venezuela the political thinking is reflected in practice. Various levels and natures of restrictions are placed on the NGOs either overtly or covertly. It is therefore important that NGO leadership is aware of the legal and political environment it is operating in.

Most of the cases where there are restrictions, it has to do with regimes being suspicious of foreign sources of funding or just blocking NGO growth knowing that most projects with larger budgets are supported by foreign funding. Partly this explains the notion of the syndrome among most indigenous NGOs relying on foreign funding. It is the belief of the author that amidst adversity, the most brilliant innovations come to the surface. This is however the work of positive mentality. Except for the case of the category of associations in Indonesia, the issue of NGOs engaging in commercial activity does not seem to come across as restricted by law or practice. The phenomenal imagination and practices of BRAC and other NGOs discussed herein are testimony that NGOs can raise substantial funds domestically.

Chapter Six

Areas that NGOs Should Work On

Most indigenous NGOs are in situations where their capacities are limited in as far as resource mobilization as championed in this book is concerned. There are various factors to the state of affairs, some out of the control of NGOs while others are within their control. In this chapter, some ideas are shared on the way forward for the NGOs. Dealing with most of the issues that are within the control of the NGOs themselves can unlock a lot of opportunities and this can easily be confirmed by the end when one finishes reading this chapter.

NGOs in the developing world generally lack clout as most of them do not have established brand names like those of the international NGOs such as OXFAM, Action Aid, World Vision or Save the Children. Of course a long history of most of these international NGOs gives them comparative advantage just as their places of origin (the West) do. The general observation is that while it may not be official among some of the western donors, they find it more convenient to trust NGOs from the west in channeling funds to the developing world than it would be with local NGOs. However this is not to say that some local NGOs do not receive funding directly from western donors. Moreover the international NGOs have better capacities in most cases to handle larger budgets than most local NGOs can do. Some of the challenges are generated within the NGOs themselves and here we examine some of the major ones:

Leadership is a major challenge in most NGOs in the developing world. For instance, most NGOs in the developing world are still suffering from what has been termed as "founder syndrome" and this has sometimes led to their stunted growth. Most NGOs start with noble causes driven by the passion of their founders, however, most of them fail to read the signs of the times or simply ignore them and continue to operate with the same mental framework they had when the organization was just beginning. Founders who move with time have a very high chance of being relevant to their organization for a very long time. Consider the case of the founder and now chairman of

BRACA, Sir Fazle Hasan Abed who was knighted after leading his organization for thirty eight years! Surely when he leaves stage, he will leave an enviable legacy worthy emulating by leadership of NGOs in the developing world. Most leaders are afraid of change and in the process they alienate a generation of professionals who would help move the organization to a different level as time goes by. This draws glaring contrasts with what has generally been the case with the international NGOs we see today, most whom got established at the end of either the First or Second World War. Examining the history of international NGOs such as OXFAM and Save the Children, one finds that their founders were driven more by passion rather than personal status. Such was the case that when two founding sisters of Save the Children, Eglantyne Jebb and Dorothy Buxton left the stage after forming the organization in 1919, their vision has survived their deaths. The same story applies to the likes of OXFAM. The challenge with most NGOs emerging out of the developing world is that they eventually are centered on personalities who cannot leave the stage when processes and trends demand so. Such founding members view the NGOs they establish as a form of pension (if retired) or as a mere source of living.

Illustrating further the opportunism of some NGO leaders, one temporarily relinquished her position to campaign for an elected position while their child took over the NGO in caretaker capacity. After failing in the election, they went back to claim their position in the NGO!

Governance for local NGOs is another aspect of leadership that faces serious constraints. The situation in most cases is that founding executive directors choose their friends and family members to sit on the NGO boards. Boards are supposed to provide guidance and oversight to the operations of NGO managements; however, by choosing close associates or soft targets, executive directors retain the powers to maneuver their way around in practice while the powers of boards only exist in theory. Besides this form of nepotism, most boards still fall short of awareness on their role in general resource mobilization for NGOs. With such situations, it is not easy to attract worthwhile funding let alone strategic guidance on effective mobilization of resources.

With time, leadership that is not foresighted becomes the dominant feature of the local NGO and there is loss of credibility in the eyes of society including the donors. As such circumstances arise, the risk of failure to raise funds increases.

Inadequate understanding of the purpose of strategic plans is another challenge faced by indigenous NGOs in the developing world. Some of them have strategic plans on paper only, and produced at the insistence of donors as a prerequisite for funding and further support. When leadership does not fully understand the rationale behind a strategic plan, they cannot guide an organization effectively, let alone on the path towards financial sustainability.

There is general lack of investment in branding as a marketing strategy. This emanates from lack of awareness and the psyche within the non for profit sector especially in the developing world that branding is the domain of the private sector which has a commercial orientation. In that respect NGOs miss the opportunity for trans-sectoral learning, which has potential to raise their profile.

Most NGOs do not have dedicated strategies on fundraising in place as a guide to inform their direction on the generation of own income. While most were almost 100% donor funded and they are constantly stationed in the vulnerable mode as far as funding is concerned, the few that engage in income generating activities do so on ad hoc basis. This is compounded by lack skills and also in most cases lack of innovation in terms of strategic fundraising e.g. project proposal writing, researching for donors and enterprise development. The result is that NGOs in the developing world are confined to surviving on limited funding sources most of which are short term and of low budgets.

Another dimension to stunted growth in terms of resource mobilization for some NGOs in the developing world is the fact that they have not really been in a situation where they are completely out of funding from donors. What this does to them is that they are comfortable even with a single low budget project as long as it represents donor presence.

Characteristics of a sustainable NGO

Having examined the various aspects on resource mobilization for NGOs in the developing world, we begin to appreciate that it is a complex (not complicated) process and requires level headedness, revisiting of the existing mental models among NGO leaders and an acceptance of a new order. It is also clear by now that applying a business model to an NGO management framework does not mean the NGO has abrogated its social responsibilities. Below we discuss a summary of what sustainable NGO should look like.

Strategy making

Having a strategic plan is very key to an organization as it provides the guiding route towards the realization of its vision. This vision has to be a shared vision within the organization and then it is translated into a strategy to operationalize it. An organization should choose its strategies depending on various factors at play. These factors include the prevailing trends in its contextual environment, also known as driving forces and have been discussed under PESTEL in chapter two. Analyzing its strengths, weaknesses, opportunities and threats (SWOT), the focus is on the resources available in terms of human; social; physical and financial capital among others. It is important for an organization that is developing a strategic plan to appreciate the prevailing conditions at the various levels in the environment and be able to relate them with its own capabilities. By developing a strategy, an NGO can be guided on the appropriate way forward and can identify what programmatic areas and business ventures to embark on.

Established constituency

An NGO should have a defined constituency with which trust should be built. Trust has to be built in terms of the work that it is doing in that constituency and the manner in which it is doing the work. The primary purpose for existence of NGOs is to facilitate change in a particular section(s) of society and the funds it accesses are acquired in the name of that constituency. It is therefore necessary that an NGO should define its group of existing or potential beneficiaries clearly. An NGO's work and approach needs to be socially and culturally acceptable to win the confidence of the constituents they serve.

Sound Organizational governance

Camay and Gordon (2002:1) define organizational governance as the manner in which power is exercised in the optimal deployment of organizational resources so as to maximally achieve the mission of the organization while Gregson (2003:2) describes it as concerning the process of agreeing the long term direction, priorities and performance of the organization and being held accountable for the use of the NGO's resources by its stakeholders. The central tenets of sound governance at NGO level are transparency and accountability. An NGO that displays transparency and accountability to its stakeholders has a greater chance of becoming financially sustainable because it commands goodwill that can generate confidence among the stakeholders to provide support or champion its cause. A transparent and accountable organization also understands the relevant legislation to guide its operations. To achieve this, an organization should have an effective governance oversight function through having a board of governors who have passion for NGO work, be well versed with the concept of organizational governance and are willing to make time for the NGO through on going support and direction to management.

Enlightened management

Just like a sound organizational governance system is key for oversight, an enlightened management will ensure that implementation of strategy is effective and efficient. In line with the discipline of personal mastery, management should work towards refining its skills in the running of the organization and providing leadership to staff. Allocating and utilizing resources effectively for programme delivery and business investment is an important function reflecting an enlightened management.

Learning culture

For an organization to be to able to read the environment and see the opportunities and potential obstacles, it has to be a learning organization. A learning organization establishes mechanisms for feedback processes at various levels. It is through appropriate feedback processes that a platform for improvement can be established.

External and public relations

An NGO should establish good external relations with other organizations, government and the public at large. When an organization enjoys sound relations with other organizations and the general public, it cultivates a sense of goodwill, as social capital from which it can derive many benefits including acquisition for support of its cause. This is achieved through creation of an image or picture that is appealing among those groups of individuals or organizations. A clear strategy on managing external and public relations is fundamental for an NGO that is serious about achieving financial autonomy.

Table 10 below summarises the discussion on prerequisites for financial autonomy

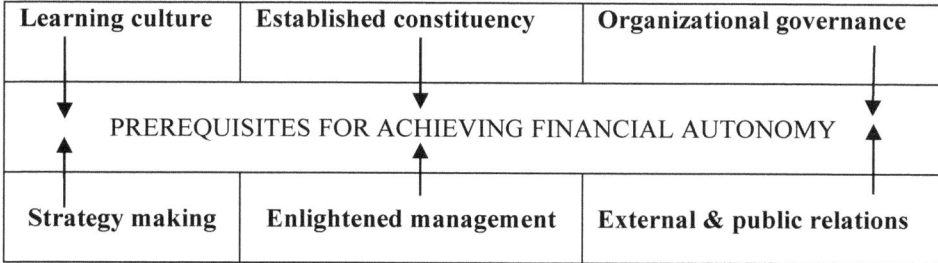

Learning culture	Established constituency	Organizational governance
PREREQUISITES FOR ACHIEVING FINANCIAL AUTONOMY		
Strategy making	Enlightened management	External & public relations

The core discussion in this chapter is change. This is change at a broader organizational development level but centered in the change of mindset by the leadership. In the next paragraph, the chapter is closing with some tips for leadership in indigenous NGOs.

In this journey of change, an effective leader must look inside himself or herself first. He or she must understand himself or herself first and acknowledge that he or she does not have all the knowledge. This acknowledgement is fundamental and empowering to the leader and his or her followers and can only be achieved if the leader understands what he or she knows and can do and what he or she cannot. It is also necessary for the leader to be aware and accept unconditionally that followers make leaders successful. When they are convinced that you are the type of leader worthy following, they will avail their genuine loyalty to you, they will avail their skills and knowledge. That will enable you to lead in the resource mobilization drive taking your organization into a progressive future.

Chapter Seven

Conclusion

We all acknowledge the tremendous role that NGOs play in society where in some cases they completely take over aspects of social service from governments where the public social service system has collapsed. The important role of traditional donors can also not be underestimated. NGOs in the developing world continue to rely heavily on such donors. However we are all aware that such financial support does not come on a silver platter and has its own limitations in terms of autonomy for NGOs. Experience over the years has revealed that

- Donors' behavior is unpredictable
- Heavy reliance on a single donor is potentially catastrophic
- Conditions set out by donors may undermine the autonomy of NGO and its purpose
- There is bias towards projects neglecting the organizations that implement them

Under these circumstances most NGOs find themselves placed in awkward situations and become vulnerable. It should be acknowledged however that it is not all donors that place strict conditions and also that it is not necessarily bad to attach conditions to funding because this enhances accountability on the part of the beneficiary NGOs. The issue here is the excessive conditions placed by some donors which completely render NGOs sovereignty impossible.

It is time for NGOs in the developing world to cultivate and embrace a new thinking and practice to resource mobilization. This new thinking and practice is serious business and does not happen by accident. There is effort that has to be applied, time must be spent, skills applied and resources allocated to plan and implement resource mobilization effectively. There are various types of funding sources that NGO leadership must know, understand and examine to enable them plan appropriately. Some of these sources are very well established in the mindset of NGO leadership while others appear alien. However, the mix of the sources provides an important balance for NGO autonomy as the aspect of accessing unrestricted funds releases the NGOs from the yolk of always having to dance to the whims of those providing restricted funding.

Achieving and maintaining a funding mix balance calls for NGOs to master the art of resource mobilization in such a way that they think enterprise but act social. This book encourages NGOs to maintain relationships with traditional donors but with a new relationship framework. The relationship has to be nurtured and should be looked at as an investment and the indigenous NGOs must happen to resource mobilization and not the other way. When NGOs happen to resource mobilization, they will be in a position to make choices on which donors to partner with and which ones not to and this is very empowering.

The NGOs in the developing world must embrace the fact that engaging in commercial activity is normal for them, it is not immoral and in most legislative jurisdictions it is accommodated. The question of morality comes with the usage of the funds so generated.

In all this the fundamental shift in the prevailing mental models among the NGO leaders becomes the main deciding factor on the future of resource mobilization among the indigenous NGOs in the developing world.

Appendix 1

List of Bilateral Sources of funds for NGOs

Agencia Espanola de Cooperacion Internacional (AECI)
Australian Agency for International Development (AUSAID)
Austrian Development Agency (ADA)
Belgian Development Cooperation (DGCD)
Canadian International Development Agency
Danish International Development Agency
Department for International Development (DfID)
Deutsche Gesellschaft fur Technische Zusammenarbeit (GTZ)
Development Cooperation Finland
Flanders International Co-operation Agency (FICA)
French Development Agency (AFD)
French Global Environmental Facility (FFEM)
Hellenic Aid (Greece)
IrishAid
Cooperazione allo Sviluppo (Italie)
Japan International Cooperation Agency (JICA)
Netherlands Development Assistance
New Zealand's International Aid and Development Agency (NZAID)
Norwegian Agency for Development Cooperation (NORAD)
Swedish International Development Agency (SIDA)
Swiss Agency for Development Cooperation (SDC)
United States Agency for International Development (USAID)
United States Department of State

List of Multilateral Sources of funds for NGOs

Africa Capacity Building Foundation (ACBF)
African Development Bank (AfDB)
Asian Development Bank (ADB)
Communities and Small Scale Mining
Consultative Group to Assist the Poorest (CGAP)
Development Marketplace

EuropeAid
Global Environmental Facility (GEF)
Global Fund to Fight HIV/AIDS, Tuberculosis and Malaria
InfoDev: ICT Development Funds for NGOs
Post Conflict Fund
Preston Fund for Girls Education
United Nations Development Programme (UNDP)
World Bank
World Bank's Girls Education Fund
World Bank's Information Technology Funds
World Bank's NGO Capacity Building Funds
World Bank's Partnership for Capacity Building Program in Africa

List of Foundations

ABILIS Foundation
Aga Khan Foundation
American Jewish World Service
American-Himalayan Foundation
Ananda Foundation
Andrew W. Mellon Foundation
Asia Foundation
Barrow Cadbury Foundation
Baxter International Foundation
Belinda Stronach Foundation
Bernard van Leer Foundation
Better World Together Foundation
Big Lottery Foundation
Bill and Melinda Gates Foundation
Blaustein Philanthropic Group
Brian Bronfman Family Foundation
CAFOD
Channel Foundation
Charles Stewart Mott Foundation
Children's Investment Fund Foundation
Christian Aid
Comic Relief
Commonwealth Foundation
Conservation Food and Health Foundation
Cottonwood Foundation

David and Barbara B.Hirschhorn Foundation
Fig Tree Foundation
First Hand Foundation
Ford Foundation
Foundation for Future
Freedom to Create
Freudenberg Foundation
Fund for Global Human Rights
Global Fund for Children
Global Fund for Women
Global Greengrants Fund
Grassroots International
Henry and Ruth Blaustein Rosenberg Foundation
ICCO
Intel Corporation
International Reading Association
Inter-American Foundation
Izumi Foundation
Jacob and Hilda Blaustein Foundation
Joseph Rowntree Charitable Trust
John Merck Foundation
Kehanoff Foundation
KIOS
King Baudouin Foundation
Lemelson Foundation
Libra Foundation
M.A.C AIDS Fund
MacArthur Foundation
Mama Cash
MckNight Foundation
Means to Live Foundation
Merill Lynch
Microsoft's NGO Connection
Minor Foundation
Monsanto Foundation
Morton K and Jane Blaustein Foundation
New Field Foundation

New World Foundation
Norwegian Human Rights Fund
Onaway Trust
One Woman Initiative
Open Society Institute
Packard Foundation
Partnership for Transparency Fund
Paul Hamlyn Foundation
Peace and Development Fund
Peacock Foundation
Presbyterian Hunger Program
Rabobank Foundation
Rockefeller Brothers Fund
Rockefeller Foundation
Sasakawa Peace Fundation
Shuttleworth Foundation
Sigrid Rausing Trust
Sir Harry Steward Trust
Starbucks Social Entrepreneurs Fund
Steven Lewis Foundation
Surdna Foundation
Taiwan Foundation for Democracy
Toyota Foundation
Trusthouse Charitable Foundation
United States Institute of Peace
Virtual Foundation
Western Union Fund
WINGS Global Fund for Community Foundations
W.K Kellogg Foundation

REFERRENCES

An interview with Fazle Hasan Abed, viewed 16 February 2011 <www.jessicamuddit.wordpress.com>

D'Souza, A 1997, Child Relief and You-Cry (India), The Synergos Institute viewed 10 March 2011, <http://www.synergos.org

Fowler, A 1997, Striking a balance, Earthscan, London

Friends of AIDS Support Trust (FAST), 2009, Fundraising and resource mobilisation strategy (2010-2014)

Government of Malawi, 2000, *NGO Act*, viewed 26 September 2006, <http://www.sdnp.org.mw>

Graham, K & Ngwende, D 1998, An introduction to basic principles of fundraising, proceedings of a fundraising workshop

Hartman, H 2007, What is the stock market? viewed 7 March 2011, <http://www.factmonster.com>

How to start an endowment for your nonprofit, viewed 8 March 2011, <http://www.nonprofit.about.com>

http://www.acf.org.uk, viewed 13 March 2011

http://www.brac.net, viewed 16 February 2011

http://www.cafod.org.uk, viewed 18 February 2011

http://www.charityvillage.com, viewed 13 March 2011

http://www.cry.org, viewed 10 March 2011

http://www.economics-dictionary.com, viewed 13 March 2011

http://www.en.wikipedia.org, viewed 13 March 2011

http://www.environment-integration.eu, viewed 13 March 2011

http://www.fica.be, viewed 13 March 2012

http://www.fundsforngos.org, viewed 13 March 2011

http://www.guardian.co.uk, viewed 22 December 2010

http://www.ibase.br, viewed 16 February 2011

http://www.icnl.org, viewed 19 February 2011

http://www.investopedia.com, viewed 8 March 2011

http://www.jstor.org/stable/3993307, viewed 9 March 2011

http://www.members.fortunecity.com/tacdrup/about.html, viewed13 March 2011

http://www.mountmulanje.org.mw, viewed 13 May 2012
http://www.networkingaction.net, viewed 23 February 2011
http://www.nonprofitexpert.com, viewed 13 March 2011
http://www.oxfam.org.uk, viewed 22 December 2010
http://www.philrice.gov, viewed 9 March 2011
http://www.resource-alliance.org, viewed 9 March 2011
http://www.savethechildren.org.uk, viewed 22 December 2010
http://www.tnm.co.mw, viewed 10 March 2011
http://www.wikipedia.org, viewed 16 February 2011
http://www.worldvision.com.au, viewed 13 May 2012
http://www.x-rates.com, viewed 16 March 2011
http://www.yoneco.org, viewed 10 March 2011
IBASE, a short story, viewed 17 February 2011, <www.wordpress.com>
Kapyepye, M 2009, An *assessment of the applicability of business strategy approaches to achieve greater financial autonomy in the local non governmental organisation sector in Malawi:* A case of the Active Youth Initiative for Social Enhancement (AYISE), Masters Dissertation submitted to the University of Kwa Zulu Natal

Mango, 2005, Sources of funding, Mango's guide to financial management for NGOs viewed 22 February 2008, <http://www.mango.org.uk/guide/files/sources-of-funding.doc>
Memorandum of Understanding (2008-2011), TNM and YONECO
Minch, KJ 2005, Bilateral vs multilateral Aid, viewed 13 March 2011, <www.idebate.org>
Mulanje Mountain Conservation Trust (2010), Annual report 2009-2010
Regional Partnership for Resource Development, 2009, Resource mobilization for sustainability proceedings of International Conference on Resource Mobilisation
Serrano, L 2007, Amanco: providing irrigation systems to the rural poor, viewed 10 March 2011, <http://www. growinginclusivemarkets.org>

TVM news at 8 2006, television programme, Malawi television, Blantyre, 19 September.

100

Waddell, S 2002, Core competencies: a key force in business-government-civil society collaborations, Journal of corporate citizenship, autumn, Issue 7 pp 43-57

Zamorano, AO 1997, Foundation for Higher Education (Colombia) (Fundacion para la Educacion Superior – FES), The Synergos Institute, viewed 10 March 2011 <http://www.synergos.org>

Index